The Paralegal's Handbook

IS LAW SCHOOL THE NEXT STEP IN YOUR LEGAL CAREER?

Consider the advantages you already possess as a paralegal:

- You have real-world experience with clients, research, and the day-to-day practicalities of law.
- You have a network of contacts within the legal profession beyond that of many law students.
- You know the satisfaction of helping people resolve their legal issues.

To find out more about law school, the LSAT, and the application process, visit *www.kaptest.com/practice* or call **1-800-KAP-TEST**.

The Paralegal's Handbook

PUBLISHING

New York

This publication is designed to provide accurate and authoritative information in regard to the subject matter covered. It is sold with the understanding that the publisher is not engaged in rendering legal, accounting, or other professional service. If legal advice or other expert assistance is required, the services of a competent professional should be sought.

© 2008 Anita Haworth & Lesley Cox

Published by Kaplan Publishing, a division of Kaplan, Inc.
1 Liberty Plaza, 24th Floor
New York, NY 10006

Printed in the United States of America

July 2008
10 9 8 7 6 5 4 3 2 1

ISBN-13: 978-1-4277-9705-6

Kaplan Publishing books are available at special quantity discounts to use for sales promotions, employee premiums, or educational purposes. Please email our Special Sales Department to order or for more information at kaplanpublishing@kaplan.com, or write to Kaplan Publishing, 1 Liberty Plaza, 24th Floor, New York, NY 10006.

Table of Contents

Chapter 1

Overview of Paralegal Practice

WHAT IS A PARALEGAL? The National Federation of Paralegal Associations (NFPA) defines a paralegal as "a person, qualified through education, training or work experience to perform substantive legal work that requires knowledge of legal concepts and is customarily, but not exclusively, performed by a lawyer. This person may be retained or employed by a lawyer, law office, governmental agency or other entity or may be authorized by administrative, statutory or court authority to perform this work. Substantive shall mean work requiring recognition, evaluation, organization, analysis, and communication of relevant facts and legal concepts."

The American Bar Association (ABA) defines a paralegal/legal assistant as "a person, qualified by education, training or work experience who is employed or retained by a lawyer, law office, corporation, governmental agency or other entity and who performs specifically delegated substantive legal work for which a lawyer is responsible."

So what does this really mean? It means that a paralegal often does many things that, *but for* the paralegal, would be done by the attorney. No matter what area of law, paralegals are often the front line with clients and witnesses; and, in litigation cases, paralegals frequently interact with court personnel, opposing counsel, and experts. Paralegals also spend a great amount of time drafting correspondence and various other documents including, but not limited to, pleadings, motions and briefs, discovery requests and responses, contracts, and exhibits. Consequently, excellent written and verbal communication skills are essential. Paralegals may perform legal research, create presentations, and file documents electronically. It is vitally important that the paralegal be able to work with many types of software programs and, in many instances, also be able to set up or troubleshoot the hardware involved. As the courts and all working environments become more dependent on technology, it is the paralegal that combines traditional paralegal skills with technological knowledge who will be most sought after.

A paralegal must be flexible, organized, and efficient. No matter what the area of law, a paralegal must often juggle multiple projects while keeping track of, and meeting, deadlines associated with each. It is common to be stopped in the middle of a project in order to handle something else that the attorney or client wants done right away. This necessitates that the paralegal be able to multitask and keep track of the status of several projects simultaneously.

UTILIZATION

As with many other professions, the paralegal profession has evolved from one that was primarily an apprenticeship to one that now requires at least a certain amount of education in order to be considered a valid candidate for the job. It would be very rare in this day and age for an individual to be hired without any education and/or training as a paralegal. Years ago, however, it was common to work one's way into a paralegal position. Most paralegals were formerly legal secretaries who had a great deal of experience and legal savvy and could be counted on to draft accurate discovery responses, pleadings, and the like for the attorney. This person had usually worked for that attorney for several years and was given increased responsibility as the attorney became familiar with his or her skills and knowledge of the law.

Through the years, specific paralegal education programs developed with the intent to teach lay persons the knowledge and skills necessary to obtain a paralegal position. There are now certificate programs, associate's degrees, bachelor's degrees, and even master's programs in paralegal studies. It is no longer necessary for employers to teach or train someone from the ground up. Employers today want and expect the person they hire as a paralegal to have the education and training (and often the experience) necessary to do the tasks assigned to him or her.

Paralegals work in all areas of the law; they can be employed by law firms, municipalities, and county, state, and federal government offices. They can work for prosecutors, public defenders, and legal aid societies, at financial institutions, for property management companies, insurance companies, and in all types of corporate legal departments. Paralegals can also work for philanthropic societies, nonprofit organizations, or private individuals. Sole practitioners and small, medium, and large law firms all utilize paralegals.

What a paralegal actually does greatly depends on the environment in which the paralegal works. For instance, in some of the smaller law firms, the paralegal will normally do all of his or her own correspondence and typing. In addition, in a smaller law firm, the paralegal is more likely to work on a variety of cases and in multiple areas of the law. In larger law firms, the paralegal is more likely to have a secretary and work in more specialized areas of law or in a particular court system. For instance, a paralegal may specialize in patent/trademark, intellectual property, or federal litigation. Corporate paralegals may work in the litigation section or in corporate finance, mergers and acquisitions, or contracts. Governmental paralegals will also have varied responsibilities depending on the particular section of government for which they work, which could be regulatory, legislative, or other.

One of the most important skills a paralegal can have is the ability to write well. A paralegal must write letters, memoranda, and all types of correspondence. Accurate knowledge of English grammar and an ability to spell are essential (spell-checker will catch many errors but not all!). It is vital to remember that the paralegal's work product affects the reputation of both the employer and the client, and a poorly written document will reflect poorly upon the attorney and upon the client's case.

It is also important to know how to perform legal research and analysis. Despite the fact that law clerks or associates might do most of the research, a paralegal often needs to be able to locate and/or review an opinion for its applicability to the current case and to know how to properly cite it in briefs and memoranda. Consequently, a paralegal should be able to utilize both electronic and traditional methods of legal research.

Competency and professionalism are two of the most important elements for a paralegal to have. Competency involves knowledge, experience, and the ability to apply that knowledge and experience to a particular task or set of tasks. Education leads to knowledge and is the essential first step to becoming a paralegal. Education provides a foundation upon which to build your knowledge through the application of what has been learned. By applying what you have learned, you gain the skills and experience to become competent. Remember that education does not end upon graduation but continues throughout your lifetime. To remain competent, you have an obligation to continually strive to maintain and increase your knowledge of the law and changes in the law, so that you can apply that knowledge to the work at hand. This increased knowledge may be gained by attending continuing legal education seminars, networking with other legal professionals, and actively participating in a paralegal professional organization.

A paralegal performs substantive legal work that involves legal concepts and is customarily (but not exclusively) performed by a lawyer. Lawyers must attend college, then law school, and pass a bar exam in order to become licensed to practice law. It therefore stands to reason that paralegals should also have an advanced education and meet certain minimum criteria in order to perform the substantive tasks delegated by the attorney.

Integrity and maturity are essential to professionalism. Adherence to and understanding of the code of ethics of the paralegal's professional association and of the attorney's ethical obligations and professional responsibilities are basic to becoming a professional. Respect for the law and for the tribunal process is absolutely necessary. Personal conduct must reflect high moral and ethical standards in both public and private situations. A paralegal must know and respect the boundaries in which the paralegal performs legal services and must know when and how to perform the duties given so as to avoid even the *appearance* of an impropriety. For example, there is a fine line between providing information and giving legal advice, and sometimes it takes time and experience to know the difference. This takes us back to the point that education provides a foundation. Each person then has an obligation to build on that foundation through experience in order to gain competency and become a professional.

One last point to make is that there is a difference between belonging to a profession and being a professional. Graduating from a paralegal program and then being hired as a paralegal may bring you into the profession, but being a professional means making a commitment to yourself to grow and learn, to adhere to standards of conduct, and to respect the law. It means incorporating these values and tenets into a way of life.

Consequently, one's competency and professionalism may well determine how one is utilized as a paralegal. Having the knowledge and experience to undertake a particular legal task, as well as an understanding of the ethical obligations and responsibilities that go along with it, is more likely to result in challenging and interesting work.

ETHICAL RESPONSIBILITIES OF PARALEGALS

Check your state and local rules for specific rules and regulations regarding nonlawyer assistants. Some states regulate the paralegal profession in some fashion, others do not. Some states have adopted rules or guidelines that apply to paralegals. Professional associations may also have codes of professional responsibility for their members. Many states have looked to the ABA for guidelines. Paralegals have the same professional and ethical responsibilities as attorneys; however, while paralegals are allowed to perform many tasks under the supervision of an attorney, they are not licensed to practice law, and there are certain things that they are not permitted to do.

Generally, a lawyer may not delegate the following to a nonlawyer:
- Responsibility for establishing an attorney/client relationship
- Responsibility for establishing the amount of a fee to be charged for a legal service
- Responsibility for a legal opinion rendered to a client

Many books have been written on the subjects of ethics and professional responsibility as they apply to paralegals that can provide a more comprehensive discussion. This section provides an overview of some important concepts of which you should be aware.

Paralegals should be familiar with the rules of professional responsibility that apply to both attorneys and paralegals generally and in specific jurisdictions. The following resources may be helpful:
- American Bar Association Model Rules of Professional Conduct (*www.abanet.org/cpr/mrpc*)
- American Bar Association Model Guidelines for Utilization of Paralegal Services (*www.abanet.org/cpr/mrpc*)
- National Federation of Paralegal Associations Code of Ethics and Professional Responsibility (*www.paralegals.org*)
- National Association of Legal Assistants Model Standards and Guidelines for Utilization of Legal Assistants/Paralegals (*www.nala.org*)

Confidentiality Rules

- *Ethical.* Conforming to the standards imposed by the ethical codes in place in the state in which the attorney practices law.
- *Confidentiality.* The ethical rule imposed upon an attorney or any legal professional to keep the legal professional from revealing any information about the client.
- *Attorney/client privilege.* The legal doctrine that prohibits an attorney who represents a client from testifying in open court and revealing the secrets of the client.
- *Work-product doctrine.* The legal doctrine that protects documents prepared in anticipation of litigation from being disclosed to the adversary.
- *Privilege.* A particular and peculiar benefit or advantage enjoyed by a person or corporation, beyond the common advantages of other citizens.
- *Privileged communications.* Those statements, made by certain persons within a relationship, that the law protects from forced disclosure.
- *Legal advice.* Advice that is given exclusively by those licensed to practice law, about legal matters, to clients.

One of the principle tenets of the legal profession is the rule of confidentiality of communications between clients and attorneys. The purpose of the rule is to encourage persons consulting attorneys to have honest and complete communication, which affords the client the best representation possible. The rule of confidentiality precedes the signing of a fee agreement or payment of a retainer. The rule applies not only to attorneys but to paralegals and all other employees. Confidentiality is not only a good rule of law office practice, it is an obligation to a client.

There are few exceptions to the rules requiring that any information relating to the representation of a client be kept confidential. In these limited circumstances, attorneys and paralegals may be required to reveal information.

The ABA's Model Rules of Professional Conduct Rule 1.6 provides that:

(a) A lawyer shall not reveal information relating to the representation of a client unless the client gives informed consent, the disclosure is impliedly authorized in order to carry out the representation or the disclosure is permitted by paragraph (b).

(b) A lawyer may reveal information relating to the representation of a client to the extent the lawyer reasonably believes necessary:

  (1) to prevent reasonably certain death or substantial bodily harm;

  (2) to prevent the client from committing a crime or fraud that is reasonably certain to result in substantial injury to the financial interests or property of another and in furtherance of which the client has used or is using the lawyer's services;

  (3) to prevent, mitigate, or rectify substantial injury to the financial interests or property of another that is reasonably certain to result or has resulted from the client's commission of a crime or fraud in furtherance of which the client has used the lawyer's services;

  (4) to secure legal advice about the lawyer's compliance with these Rules;

  (5) to establish a claim or defense on behalf of the lawyer in a controversy between the lawyer and the client, to establish a defense to a criminal charge or civil claim against the lawyer based upon conduct in which the client was involved, or to respond to allegations in any proceeding concerning the lawyer's representation of the client; or

  (6) to comply with other law or a court order.

Confidentiality rules encompass the attorney/client privilege and work-product doctrines, but the confidentiality rules extend far beyond those evidentiary rules and may come into play at any time (not merely before a tribunal). Confidentiality rules increase the types of matters that may not be revealed by a client's attorney and protect more information than that which is protected by attorney/client privilege.

Attorney/client privilege and the work-product doctrine are evidentiary rules that apply in limited situations. They are meant to protect from disclosure what might otherwise become evidence during litigation proceedings. Attorney/client privilege prohibits the attorney and paralegal from testifying or otherwise revealing the secret of a client. The work-product doctrine protects documents prepared in anticipation of litigation from being disclosed to an adversary. While these rules protect confidential information of a client from being disclosed during litigation proceedings, the ethical rule of confidentiality protects information from being disclosed at any time.

Paralegals should preserve all confidential information provided by the client or acquired from other sources before, during, and after the course of the professional relationship. Information learned even after the representation of the client has concluded should be kept confidential even though this information may have come from a third party. It is a good rule of practice to avoid speaking with third parties about any representation of clients, thus preventing inadvertent disclosures. You should avoid talking about your cases. If you are meeting or talking on the telephone with a client, do so in private. Avoid talking on cell phones about confidential client matters. Protect your computer screen from view so that client information is not revealed. If you are preparing a response to a Request for Production, avoid producing documents that are confidential or are the attorney's work-product. Confidentiality is one of the most important ethical rules. Paralegals must be aware of this rule and be diligent in protecting the client's interests.

UNAUTHORIZED PRACTICE OF LAW

Unauthorized practice of law (UPL) has been defined as nonlawyers engaging in activities that only lawyers are licensed and sanctioned to perform. While this is a general definition, the unauthorized practice of law is specifically prohibited. It is against the law for someone who is not an attorney to practice law. This includes assisting someone in the unauthorized practice of law.

Definitions
- *Practice of law.* An activity involving the exercise of independent legal judgment, such as advising clients and representing clients in court.
- *Independent legal judgment.* Judgment that is exercised by those educated in the law; the application of a general body of law to a specific factual situation; advising clients and representing them in court or before other tribunals; drafting and signing papers.
- *Attorney/client relationship.* The relationship between retained counsel and a client that encompasses privileges of communications, legal advice, and representation. This is considered a fiduciary relationship. While an attorney may ethically delegate many tasks to a paralegal, the attorney has an obligation to maintain a direct relationship with a client.

Paralegals must avoid exercising independent legal judgment. Therefore, paralegals should not give clients legal advice. However, the paralegal may relay the lawyer's legal advice to the client, clearly stating that this is the lawyer's advice and being very careful not to expand on that advice.

Likewise, the paralegal may prepare legal documents, pleadings, and discovery for the attorney's review and signature. By reviewing and signing the documents, the attorney is acknowledging the work product as his or her own, completed as part of the attorney's representation of the client.

By failing to participate in the process, the attorney is essentially giving the exercise of independent legal judgment to the paralegal. The paralegal is then engaging in the unauthorized practice of law, and the attorney is assisting in the unauthorized practice of law.

Courts have held that it is not necessary for an individual to state or imply that he or she is a lawyer for courts to find that the practice of law exists. It is not necessary to collect fees to be engaged in the practice of law.

In some instances, paralegals may represent clients before certain federal and state administrative agencies. It is very important that you check with the agency in the specific jurisdiction to make that determination.

While attorneys ultimately are responsible for the actions of paralegals, paralegals must take care to understand the limits of their responsibilities so they do not mistakenly engage in the practice of law. Attorneys and paralegals must be diligent in identifying the paralegal as such, explaining that the paralegal is not licensed to practice law. If a paralegal's name appears on a firm's letterhead or business cards, he or she must be identified as a paralegal. Attorneys may charge for the work performed by paralegals but may not split fees with paralegals. An attorney may compensate a paralegal based on the quantity and quality of the paralegal's work and the value of that work to a law practice, but the paralegal's compensation may not be contingent, by advance agreement, on the profitability of the attorney's practice.

It can be particularly difficult for paralegals to avoid the unauthorized practice of law; therefore, it is essential for all paralegals to remain diligent in their efforts to do so.

Chapter 2

Investigation and Fact Gathering

THE BASICS

A **PARALEGAL IS OFTEN CALLED** on to investigate and gather facts. Where to look and what to look for will vary depending on the type of case and area of law involved. There are specific questions that must be answered first in order to determine what to look for. These main questions, shown below, will be the same no matter what area of law is involved:

- WHO are the parties involved?
  - Plaintiff/Defendant
  - Husband/Wife
  - Buyer/Seller
  - Debtor/Creditor
  - Witnesses
  - Other

- WHAT occurred (or did *not* occur that was *supposed* to)?
- WHEN did the incident occur or what is the time period involved?
- WHERE
  - Did the matter take place?
  - Was each party at the time of occurrence?
  - Was each witness?
- WHY
  - Did this happen (or *not* happen if it was *supposed* to)?
  - Are the parties important?
  - Is the time/time period important?
  - Is the location important/not important?
- HOW did this occur?

In order to investigate a matter and gather facts, you must first determine what you know and what you need to know. Start by making a list of known facts and the parties involved, including witnesses. This is essential information regardless of whether you are working on a corporate merger or a personal injury case. Then make a list of information you need but do not have. Rarely will you be able to answer who, what, when, where, why, and how in the very early stages of a new case. Be sure to review all of the case notes from the attorney and all of the information provided by the client, noting that which answers your questions and that which brings up even more questions. These steps will help you to focus your efforts and be more productive.

EXAMPLE 1

Client: John B. Doe, deceased
- DOB: 12/24/1983
- FACT: Date of Accident: Friday, June 12, 2007
- FACT: Driver of 2002 Ford Escape, black, 4WD, VIN: _____
- FACT: Southbound on Interstate 40 in right-hand lane, just past on-ramp from Highway 19, when struck from behind by 18-wheeler at approximately 4:30 P.M.
- FACT: Clear, dry day

(continued)

EXAMPLE 1 (*continued*)

- FACT: After impact, Doe lost control and Escape went off right-hand side of interstate and rolled three times.
- FACT: Doe was thrown from vehicle and died at scene.
- FACT: Speed limit for cars at that point is 55 mph.
- Unknown: Was Doe wearing seat belt or did it fail?
- Unknown: How fast was Doe going?
- Unknown: Did Doe pull out in front of the 18-wheeler?
- Unknown: Was Doe under the influence of drugs or alcohol?

Defendant: James R. Jones
- DOB: 5/08/1972
- FACT: Driver of 18-wheeler that struck client
- FACT: Southbound on Interstate 40 in right-hand lane
- FACT: Struck 2002 Ford Escape, and then jackknifed into median.
- FACT: Owner-operator of the 18-wheeler
- FACT: Leased to World's Greatest Trucking Company, Detroit, MI.
- FACT: Blood alcohol test taken at the scene showed .11 and legal limit is .1.
- FACT: Speed limit for trucks at that point is 55 mph.
- Unknown: When did Jones last drink?
- Unknown: Why did the vehicles collide?
- Unknown: Was anything restricting his vision?
- Unknown: Did Jones change lanes just before the collision?
- Unknown: How fast was Jones going?

Witness 1: Suzy Sunshine
- DOB: 3/23/1949
- Address: 132 Big Dog Lane, Anytown, USA
- FACT: Driver of 2007 Cadillac Seville
- FACT: Southbound on Interstate 40 traveling in left-hand lane and behind 18-wheeler
- FACT: Did not see 2002 Ford Escape, but did see 18-wheeler brake, swerve, and then jackknife.
- FACT: Heard noise and saw 2002 Ford Escape rolling down embankment.
- FACT: Stopped to see if she could help.
- FACT: Retired nurse
- FACT: Gave statement to police.

(*continued*)

EXAMPLE I (*continued*)

Witness 2: Lazy Larry
- DOB: 8/19/1980
- Address: 515 Little Dog Lane, Anytown, USA
- FACT: Taxi driver
- FACT: Southbound on Interstate 40 in lane behind 18-wheeler
- FACT: Was preparing to exit onto Highway 19 toward airport.
- FACT: Saw 18-wheeler start to swerve left, then heard noise and saw 2002 Ford Escape go off the Interstate to the right and roll down embankment.
- FACT: Saw 18-wheeler jackknife into median.
- FACT: Stopped and gave statement to police.

Witness 3: Bob Business
- DOB: Unknown
- Address: 888 Shoreline Drive, Big City, CA
- FACT: Was checking emails.
- FACT: Just left sales meeting and was heading to airport for flight home.
- FACT: Heard screeching noise.
- FACT: Looked up and saw 18-wheeler going into median, saw Ford Escape rolling down embankment.

There are several excellent case management programs that will assist the legal team in organizing relevant information and facts for a particular area of law. Specifically, case management software provides a way to organize information so that all members of the legal team can have access to the information contained in it at any time. Such software will include sections on facts, people, and objects (including but not limited to documents, recordings, photographs, X-rays, etc.) and will allow for the creation of reports, graphs, and charts for use in meetings and at trial.

Resources

Now that you have organized the information you currently have and made note of what you need to know, you should consider the available resources. Who or what can provide you with the information you are lacking? Additional sources of information can include people, places, documents, and things.

In thinking of people as resources, be sure to include any individual that makes sense to the particular type of case. In every case, the client and the opposing party, as well as any third party who may have relevant information or information that will lead to relevant information, should be considered resources. Then think about anyone with whom these individuals have had contact. For example, in a personal injury case, you should consider family, friends, witnesses, police, medical personnel/EMTs, teachers, supervisors, coworkers, and experts—all of whom may have information that is relevant. Alternately, any of these individuals may be able to point you toward other sources of information.

Places can provide information as well. Consider the scene of a crime. When a police officer or detective investigates a crime, the crime scene includes not only the actual location of the crime but also the victim's and perpetrator's paths to and from the place where the incident occurred. Crime scene investigators look not only for trace evidence such as hair, blood, and fingerprints but also for fibers, mud, and other matter brought to the scene or carried away from it by the victim or the perpetrator. In civil cases, places can also be sources of information. Again, consider a personal injury case. The scene of the personal injury is often photographed from several different angles. This helps to determine what happened or why and whether it could actually have occurred the way it was described. Was there something that obscured one party's view that may have contributed to the accident? Was there a third party involved? If so, where was that party located at the time of the incident? Where was the client and where was the opposing party? When reviewing the location of the incident, you should determine all of the factors that may have contributed to the incident and make a note of those factors that should be ruled out. Be sure to consider also such factors as the time of year, the time of day, the lighting conditions, and the weather.

Documents are invaluable sources of information. Documents include both physical and electronic instruments. They not only provide important information but also help to verify information already provided by people. Types of documents that may be helpful in gathering facts include such things as medical, financial, Social Security, education, and employment records; property reports; income tax statements; loan applications; courthouse dockets; driver's license records; criminal histories; and other public records. Many different types of records can be obtained if you have the resources and are willing to pay a fee. For instance, a medical provider may, pursuant to specific guidelines, provide records for your client or the opposing party. However, there will be a fee involved, and the fee may be assessed pursuant to specific statutory requirements. You can also obtain such things as verified weather reports for a particular geographic location.

Another source of important documents is the government. Much information is available pursuant to the Freedom of Information Act. Specific information regarding the Freedom of Information Act can be found at *www.usdoj.gov/oip.* Administrative regulations can be obtained as well. For instance, if you go to *www.thecre.com\links\fedgov-links.html,* you will find a directory of links to federal government websites including such things as the Office of Management and Budget, President's Foreign Intelligence Advisory Board, Office of Science and Technology Policy, Office of the United States Trade Representatives, and many others, as well as links to all of the different departments of the federal government. These include, but are not limited to, the Departments of Agriculture, Commerce, Defense, Patent and Trademark, and so forth, with all of their subdepartments.

The Internet is also a huge source of information. You can find a great deal of information about someone simply by typing that person's name into a search engine. While the search results will likely produce much more than you need, along with some totally irrelevant information, you also might find something that could affect your case. In addition, there are many online programs that will provide specific details about an individual for a fee—provided you have a birth date or other specific information. Private investigators, for instance, use many online databases to obtain information about individuals—again, for a fee. You can also search for names of individuals holding specific licenses and the status of those licenses, for malpractice suits against medical providers or attorneys and even for real estate records. For those of you who grew up on computers, much of this will seem second nature. However, beware: Just because something is on the Internet, in newspapers, or on television, does not mean it is valid. Be sure to verify the source and make sure that the information is true.

Things that may be sources of information would include just about anything else you can think of. A newspaper archive, the Library of Congress, and even someone's personal belongings can give you information. Understanding a person's religious beliefs might help you to understand why that person behaves or thinks a certain way. Bank accounts or credit cards can be sources of information, not just because they are sources of documented cash or debt, but also because they can tell you if other individuals are listed on those accounts or when something was last purchased or deposited.

When you are investigating and searching for information, it is vitally important to be curious about everything. Anything can be a source of new information, so be sure to keep an open mind and leave any personal biases behind. At the same time, it is also very important to stay focused on the subject and not stray into areas that have no real significance to the case.

Getting to Work

Make a list or chart of the information and facts at hand, noting which of them answer the who, what, when, where, why, and how, and noting also which party or witness can verify each fact or piece of information. Then make a list of what is unknown, what requires verification, and any other potential sources of information that you want to pursue. Decide on a plan, and discuss your plan with your supervising attorney, who may have additional suggestions for you. At any rate, the attorney should always be apprised of, and approve of, what you propose to do—in advance. As you know, the first order of business when contacting a potential witness is always to identify yourself as a paralegal, working with attorney so-and-so on behalf of your client so-and-so. It is highly unethical to attempt to speak with the opposing party when that party is represented by counsel, and it also could get you fired. Even if the opposing party is not represented, err on the side of caution. Never initiate contact with the opposing party without first obtaining permission or instruction from the supervising attorney. In addition, by first speaking with the supervising attorney regarding your plan, you can avoid any potential faux pas in the event the attorney has already contacted someone, ruled something out, or made other arrangements.

EXAMPLE 2

Issue: Breach of Contract
- Company A sells its services to Company B for $20,000 per month.
- Contract is effective as of January 1, 2005.
- Duration of contract is 5 years.
- $20,000 per month payment is due on first day of each month.
- Company A sues Company B for breach of contract for failure to pay.
- Company B counterclaims against Company A for failure to perform.
- State of jurisdiction is New York—pursuant to contract.
- Suit filed on November 15, 2007.

Company A CEO—John Doe, M.B.A.
- Knowledge of: Contract issues
  - Services performed
  - Services not performed
  - Personnel involved

Company A CFO—Darren Doe, CPA
- Knowledge of: Services performed
  - Personnel involved
  - Related costs and expenses

Employees of Company A—what they were told to do/not do
  - Actions taken

Company B CEO—Joe Smith, M.B.A.
- Knowledge of: Contract issues

(continued)

EXAMPLE 2 (*continued*)

- o Services contracted
- o Services performed
- o Services not performed
- o Personnel involved

Company B CFO—Alex Alexander, CPA
- Knowledge of: Services paid for
  - o Services performed
  - o Services not performed
  - o Personnel involved

Employees of Company B—what they saw employees of Company A do/not do
- o Actions taken

Additional information needed:
- The exact services to be performed and by whom
- The date(s) on which services were begun/stopped
- Which services were performed
- Which services were not performed
- Why services were not performed/stopped
- Amount Company A claims is owed to it
- Amount Company B paid to Company A

Interviews to be performed:
- CEO of client (Company A)—attorney to perform
- CFO of client—attorney to perform
- Employees of client—paralegal

Documents to be reviewed:
- Contract
- Services Agreement
- Work detail statements
- Financial statements
- Correspondence between Company A and Company B
- Invoices
- Internal Memos
- Emails

Once the attorney has approved your plan for gathering additional facts and information, you are ready to begin. A one-on-one interview is an excellent first step in gathering additional information from the client and any witnesses. Other options can include a thorough review of documents, utilizing Internet search engines and online databases, visiting the location where the incident occurred, and perhaps even hiring professional investigators. When investigating, make an effort to think outside the box.

The Interview

For each individual you have identified as a source of information, you should now determine the particular information you believe that individual may be able to offer. To prepare for each interview, make a list of questions based on who that person is in relation to the case, and then include questions designed to obtain the information you want or need from that person. Start with very specific questions, such as name, age, date of birth, current address, relationship to the situation or parties, and so forth. From there, you should progress to open-ended questions that are designed to allow the person to tell his or her story and/or that will give you the information you need from that person. Depending on who the person is in relation to the case, you may have more or less questions of him or her. Sometimes the attorney will do the actual interview, but the paralegal will assist with drafting questions.

Start with questions designed to tell you *who* that person is, such as the following:
- What is your full name?
- What is your address?
- What is your phone number?
- What is your age and date of birth?
- What is your relationship to the client or parties (e.g., a family member, first responder, supervisor, coworker, etc.)?
- Who is your employer?
- What is your title (e.g., Patrol Officer, Fire Chief, Captain, EMT, Property Manager, and so forth)?
- What is your experience (number of years/months in that position)?

Of course, if the interview is with a family member, then that person's employer, title, and experience may not be all that relevant. However, if the client was injured in an auto accident, and the family member is a doctor or nurse, then the family member's profession and years of experience may well be valuable as they relate to the individual's observances of the client and the client's injuries.

The next line of questioning should tell you *what* that person observed. Be sure to ask questions designed to obtain the detail needed. You will need to find out exactly what occurred or what *should have* occurred. For instance, a breach of contract often involves one party failing to perform as required, thereby causing injury to the other party. In that instance, important questions to ask are "What did the one party fail to do?" and "How was the other party injured?"

Once you have an understanding as to what occurred (or failed to occur), you need to then establish *when* it occurred. In the event it happened over a period of time, be sure to ask for the beginning and ending dates as best the person can give them. Alternately, you may need to ask questions designed to obtain dates for *each* instance that something occurred (for instance, in a sexual harassment or stalking case).

Next, proceed to questions designed around the location of the event and/or to determine proper jurisdiction. Ask *where* each party was located or where the event or series of events occurred. If there were witnesses, find out where each one was at the time of each incident. This is where a diagram or schematic is important, and details must be obtained. These can then be compared to photos of the location to determine if the party's or witness's statement is accurate. Jurisdiction is determined by the location of the event, or by the domicile of the parties. Be sure to research the Rules of Court for your particular area that will set forth the requirements for determination of jurisdiction of the court. In some instances, such as with contracts, the contract itself will indicate which state or country will have jurisdiction in regard to disputes.

The next step is to determine the *why* of the situation. For instance, why does the plaintiff believe that the defendant is responsible for the plaintiff's injuries, or why did the defendant do what he or she did? Why did the incident occur, or not, as the case may be? Perhaps there was something that interfered with the ability of one driver to see another, or perhaps one driver took his eyes off the road for some reason. It can be very difficult to get answers to all of the why questions.

Sometimes, the why and how of a situation may be the same or closely related. At other times, there may be a significant difference. For instance, you may be able to determine how an auto accident happened—the defendant crossed the center line—but *why* did this occur? It could be that the driver had a medical incident such as a heart attack or diabetic episode, was operating under the influence, or simply became distracted.

The final line of questioning should help to determine the *how*. How did the defendant breach the contract? If a product liability case, in what way did the machine fail? How did the weather contribute to the accident? How was the defendant negligent? When you have completed drafting all of the questions to be asked, have the attorney review them to offer any additions, changes, or suggestions.

When interviewing a police officer or medical personnel, be sure to keep the interview short and to the point because these individuals will often be on duty when the interview takes place. In addition, most police officers and medical personnel are loath to speculate, so questions directed to them should be *specific* and related to what they *observed*. It is acceptable, however, to ask them one or two questions designed to find out what they think about something if the questions are specifically related to an observation; for example, "You stated that there were skid marks on the road surface. Based on your knowledge and experience, do you believe those were made by the defendant's or plaintiff's vehicle?" And a follow-up question could be, "Do you have any idea how fast he or she may have been going?" Questions such as these should be asked nearer to or at the end of the interview, and again, must be specifically based on the observations made by the individual and in consideration of the individual's experience. A question like this would not be asked of a rookie police officer.

Next, consideration must be given to where the interview will take place. Will it be in person or over the telephone? Will it take place in your office or in the other person's office or home? Interviews taken over the telephone should, ideally, be short and to the point. If you are interviewing someone in his or her home or office, be observant and considerate of that person's time. When setting up the interview, be honest with the person as to how long you believe the interview will take, and try to stick to that time period. When you go to the interview, pay attention to where the witness places herself and you. There is a psychological difference between two people sitting in chairs in someone's living room versus sitting across a desk from each other or at a table. The seating arrangement could therefore affect the success or failure of the interview. When the witness comes to you for the interview, you should again consider the location and seating arrangement. Should the interview take place in your office with you sitting behind your desk (a position of power), or should it take place in a conference room with the two of you sitting at a table? This is a somewhat less formal arrangement. Another alternative is two comfortable chairs separated by an end table that puts the two of you on the same plane. Sometimes the interview will take place on neutral ground, for example, at a restaurant for lunch or over coffee.

Other important aspects of the interview include the culture and/or ethnicity and religion of the person being questioned. The witness's culture may or may not affect the interview, and what is considered commonplace behavior in the United States may well be offensive to someone from another country. Further, are you asking the person to consent to be interviewed on a religious holiday? It may be necessary to do some research so as to reduce the possibility of embarrassing or offending someone who has information that is vital to the case. Questions may need to be restated, and the seating arrangements changed. Does the person speak and understand

English fluently? If not, you may need to hire an interpreter. Be sure to do your homework here as well. Nothing could be worse than hiring the services of a bad interpreter. As for references, check with other paralegals to get referrals to good interpreters.

The goal of an interview is to get more information than is given. One of the most important things to remember when performing an interview is to *listen,* and the second most important thing is to treat the witness with the utmost respect. Remember, you represent not only your client, but also the attorney and firm for which you work. Everything you say and do will reflect upon your employer and client. You must be able to listen, because the person being interviewed may be able to provide you with information that you never expected—and that may open up a whole new line of questioning. If you are more focused on asking your questions than on what the person has to say, you could miss an important opportunity. At the same time, you also may need to draw someone back to the subject matter if the person begins to stray.

Make sure the witness is comfortable. Witnesses who are comfortable and relaxed are more likely to open up to you than those who are nervous or angry. Above all, be polite and treat the individual with respect. You never know when you may need to go back to that person for additional information, whether on this case or another, and if you are less than courteous, the witness may not bother to be available to you in the future.

During and After the Interview

There are two ways to record the information from the witness: handwritten notes or a recording device. If you intend to record the interview, you must first obtain the person's permission to do so. Once the witness approves, you can begin recording. First, state the date and time of the interview and identify all parties present. Then repeat the question to the witness about recording the interview, so that their knowledge and approval of the recording is actually part of the recording. After that, you can begin asking questions. Once the interview is over, you should label the recording and save it. Find out if the attorney wants the recorded interview transcribed or just wants a memo from you outlining the important points. In addition, if the witness asks for a copy of the transcription, be sure to provide it.

If the interview is not recorded, then the only source of information will be the notes you take. Consequently, it is imperative to be accurate, but you will need to write quickly. Be sure to repeat information or statements to the witness, or ask the witness to repeat what he or she said, if necessary, to ensure the information is correct. It is best *not* to use a laptop to take notes during the interview. Why? Because it may well be considered rude by the witness and reduce the witness's willingness to cooperate. This is especially important when the witness is of a different culture. The witness may feel he or she does not have your full attention. Even when writing notes, be sure to make eye contact with the witness. Listen to the answer, and then quickly write down what was said.

Immediately after the interview is over, draft a memo identifying the witness and describing the information obtained. The memo should be thorough yet concise. This may seem a contradiction, but it is not. The memo should begin with a paragraph identifying the witness and the date, time, and location of the interview, as well as any other person(s) present. The next paragraph(s) should describe the specific and important information obtained. Take care that you do not inadvertently substitute your impression for what the witness actually stated. Note any inconsistencies in the witness's story and anything that may be contrary to what other witnesses or the client says about the matter. A final paragraph or sentence should state whether there is any follow-up information that should be obtained from this witness and/or whether this witness identified any other sources of information. If the witness identified other sources of information, then the list or chart previously prepared will need to be updated.

It is extremely important to tell the attorney if you think the client or witness was lying, exaggerating, or guessing—but be prepared to explain why. Be sure to keep all of your notes and/or the recorded interview along with a copy of the memo in the witness's folder so that if verification of a statement in the memo is ever needed, it will be available. When working in a paperless office, all of this information will be maintained electronically.

Investigating People and Companies

A paralegal often is given the directive to find out information about a witness, expert, or the opposing party. One of the quickest and easiest ways to get information is by doing a search on the Internet. However, it is important to verify the source of any information obtained in that way because not everything on the Internet is legitimate. In addition, if you type "John Doe" into the search engine, it will not only bring up information about your "John Doe" but also about any other person with the same name. It takes time to sift through the search results to find pertinent information for your "John Doe," but if you are patient, you can sometimes locate invaluable information. This applies to companies as well as to individuals. Most expert witnesses will provide a listing of previous cases in which he or she has assisted. Check those resources by contacting the parties involved and ask their impression of the expert's services. This is imperative. Nothing could be worse than getting to court and having the opposing party debunk your expert.

Government websites are normally great sources of information and you can usually count on the information being legitimate. You can also search online telephone directories, the Bureau of Motor Vehicles (BMV), criminal court histories, sex offender registries, professional license databases, and many other online sources—both state and federal. In addition, many cities and counties have their own websites. Some of these online sources offer downloadable and certified copies of documents obtained from them—most notably, the BMV. When attempting to locate a person or to determine if a person has any property, there are companies that specialize in finding people for a fee. These fees are generally quite reasonable and run $20–$30 per search (depending on the detail requested) or involve a flat rate for a specific number of searches in a given time period. Most state courts now allow online searching of their databases for a fee, and in the federal court system, if your firm or employer already has a PACER account, you can use that account to search any federal court in any district. The U.S. Bankruptcy Court also has a searchable online database.

If you have a phone number and want to find the name or address to go with it, you can do a reverse telephone search. Several online telephone directories offer this capability. Simply type in the area code and phone number, click okay, and it will provide you with a name and address to go with that number. However, the accuracy of that information will depend on how recently the phone company's online database was updated.

The U.S. government offers a wide variety of free online information. The United States Patent and Trademark Office website, at *www.uspto.gov/main/profiles/acadres.htm*, offers detailed information on how to search for patents and trademarks using databases and links from that page. The United States Securities and Exchange Commission, at *www.sec.gov*, allows free searches of the EDGAR database, which provides detailed information regarding public companies and their filings, including names and contact information of owners and officers, and even downloadable copies of actual filings. Medline Plus, at *medlineplus.gov*, is a service of the National Library of Medicine and the National Institutes of Health. This website has information covering health topics and drugs and supplements, a medical encyclopedia and medical dictionary, news, health care provider directories, and other resources. The American Medical Association website, at *www.ama-assn.org*, also offers a provider search, a database of medical codes used in billing, a section on medical ethics and standards, and a section on health care advocacy.

Parents, siblings, friends, teachers, coworkers, and neighbors are other great resources for background information about a client or opposing party. These individuals can be interviewed rather quickly. Family members will typically be able to describe the childhood illnesses and injuries the person experienced, whether the person used drugs or was ever arrested, whether the person was a good or bad student, where the person may have worked, and other such information. Friends can tell you what some of that person's habits might have been, others that the individual might have hung out with, where that person liked to go for entertainment, and so forth. Teachers will be able to describe the individual's study habits, talents, and skills, and the students with whom the individual interacted. Neighbors can be a source of information about a person's comings and goings, habits, and perhaps idiosyncrasies. Coworkers will have impressions of a person's integrity, work ethic, habits, and depending on their relationship, might have information about the individual's family life, friends, and likes and dislikes.

Investigating the Location

As mentioned above, the location where the incident took place is important for several reasons. First, location is a determining factor in jurisdiction. When the parties are from different states or countries and the damages exceed $75,000, the matter may be filed in a federal district court. Otherwise (depending upon the type of case), it would be filed in state court. In contract law, the contract will normally specify in which state any dispute must be determined.

The location also might be important as it relates to *why* the incident occurred, and this is true when you are discussing a personal injury or product liability case, for example. For instance, an extremely humid climate might affect the internal workings of a machine causing it to malfunction, or a snowstorm could interfere with someone's ability to see the road, thereby contributing to an automobile accident. A house built in a floodplain is more likely to have water damage than one built on high ground. Consequently, location may very well be a *factor* in the case.

To assist with the investigation and fact gathering, have the client draw a diagram of the scene. The diagram should show everything the client can recall, including the location of each person, animal, and anything else. If the location is inside a building, consider the placement of the furniture, the type of flooring, lighting, and the like. If the location is outdoors, consideration must be given also to such things as the weather and the wind, time of day, shadows, trees, and buildings. Go to the scene yourself, if possible, with a copy of the client's diagram, noting where each party and any witnesses were located. Stand, sit, or lay in the same positions as each individual to determine what each would have seen. Look for anything that may have blocked their vision or affected their ability to move. Then compare the client's original diagram and your revised diagram to the client's description. What do they tell you? Do they support or controvert the information from the client? Do they provide answers or only more questions? When interviewing a significant witness, consider asking the witness to draw a diagram of the scene that shows what the witness believes occurred and how.

You may need to take photographs of the location. If so, be sure to take them from every angle, noting the position that your client, the opposing party, and any witnesses would have been in at the time. Go to the scene at the same general time of day (and time of year) that the incident occurred. You should do this fairly quickly; otherwise, things might change from when the incident occurred. Have the client review the photographs to help the client recall additional details and to determine if anything has changed. The photographs should be compared to any diagrams that were created. It is important to use a good digital camera so that the pictures will be crisp and clear. They then can be loaded on the computer for use at mediation and/or trial. In order to make use of the pictures at mediation or trial, a presentation software program is helpful.

Make notes or create a memo describing your review of the location and any significant issues it presents. Create a log of the pictures, noting the date each was taken, and include a brief description of each. This is important because it sometimes takes several months or a couple of years before mediation or trial may actually occur.

Ask the client and any witnesses if they took pictures. If so, obtain copies and go over them with the attorney. Create a log for these pictures as well, including who took them, the date(s) taken, and a brief description of each picture, and note any significance that each is expected to evidence.

Another source of information is aerial photographs. If these are needed, there are vendors who will provide them for a fee. Sometimes a local government will have taken aerial photographs as part of the planning phase for city or road development, so be sure to check all possibilities.

EXAMPLE 3

Pictures taken by Polly Paralegal with digital camera:
- Picture 1: 3/10/08, facing southbound on Interstate 40 at overpass of Highway 19; .jpg
- Picture 2: 3/10/08, facing northbound on Interstate 40 at overpass of Highway 19; .jpg
- Picture 3: 3/10/08, embankment where 2002 Ford Escape rolled down, showing damage to embankment; .jpg

Pictures taken by Deputy Smith, Johnson County Sheriff Department, June 12, 2007; Color copies:
- Picture 1: 18-wheeler jackknifed in median of Interstate 40
- Picture 2: 2002 Ford Escape at bottom of embankment, front end
- Picture 3: 2002 Ford Escape at bottom of embankment, rear end
- Picture 4: Skid marks on Interstate 40 just past on-ramp from Highway 19
- Picture 5: Damage to front end of 18-wheeler
- Picture 6: Taken at bottom of embankment facing upwards toward Interstate 40 showing damage to embankment made by Ford Escape
- Picture 7: Taken at top of embankment looking down on 2002 Ford Escape and showing damage to embankment

Investigating and Gathering Documents

There is a huge variety of documents that can be gathered during the investigation of an incident. The types of documents to be searched for will depend on the type of case and area of law. The important thing is to think about the particular case and the overall area of law, and then determine the kinds of documents you are looking for. As you begin gathering documents, be sure to keep the "originals" in pristine condition. *Never* mark up or write on originals—to do so is to destroy their validity. Instead, make working copies on which you (or the attorney) may make notes or highlight important information. If your employer utilizes a document management system, you can use the system to make notes and highlight the information you want pointed out on any particular page.

Make a list of the documents that you need to gather. Think about the types of documents that will be needed to make your client's case and/or to defend against the opposing party's case. For example, in a personal injury case, you will need to obtain the plaintiff's medical records. To determine which records to obtain, you will need to get a list of the treating physicians, hospitals, and clinics; emergency medical personnel; chiropractors; and so forth. It is important to know exactly what injuries the plaintiff sustained. In addition to any specialists, you should always plan to obtain records from the person's primary care physician, because those records may include information regarding any preexisting issues and/or will verify that no pre-existing conditions existed.

Discuss with the attorney those providers from whom you believe records should be obtained and how far back to ask for. Sometimes it is imperative to request a medical report that describes the patient's history, diagnosis, prognosis, and any expected future medical treatment that may be required as well as a statement of physical impairment. Review the medical records— these oftentimes will lead to additional information or sources of information. Medical expenses also must be verified. To do so, itemized statements will have to be collected from the various providers.

You may also need to obtain employment records, tax returns, or information pertaining to previous lawsuits, criminal convictions, or other claims for personal injury. These items are important because if someone is claiming lost wages, their employment records and tax returns will verify wages. Employment history will show what the person was able to do prior to the injury. Disability insurance information is also important because most disability insurance policies require reimbursement in the event someone receives a settlement that includes lost wages, and the subroga-tion must be paid. Previous lawsuits, criminal convictions, and other claims for personal injury are important because they relate to a person's veracity. Such records will show if there is a history of previous issues that may relate to preexisting conditions and/or a propensity to sue or claim damages or injury. While most people are inherently honest, there are those who are not—and they would use the legal system to get what they see as "easy money."

As the documents are gathered, be sure to update the list. Make a spreadsheet identifying each document, the date received, the date of the document, its author or source, and any significant information contained therein. This spreadsheet will be of great assistance later when it is time to identify exhibits for mediation or trial. In a document management system, this information is typed into specific fields within the program and becomes part of the database when the document is added to the system.

Electronic Documents

Electronic documents are another essential source of information that cannot be overlooked. There are an exponential number of electronic documents generated every day. Emails, instant messages, text messages, spreadsheets, digital photographs and videos, Web cam photos, and word processor documents, to name a few, are sometimes never printed out, but they must still be considered when gathering information. Specific considerations must be made when requesting electronically stored information (ESI), including but not limited to, the particular type of ESI to be produced, how it will be produced, in what format it will be produced, when it will be produced, the individual sources from which it will be obtained, and the particular time periods involved. The most important thing to know about ESI is when to call in the professionals—those companies that can provide services and have the knowledge and technical ability to assist in obtaining and handling electronic discovery.

Investigating Other "Things" and Sources of Information

This "miscellaneous" category represents information that can be obtained from any assortment of things that do not fall into the above categories of persons, places, or documents. For instance, what can a person's eyeglasses tell you? They will provide an indicator of how well or how badly the person can see without them—which may be significant depending on what happened. The type of clothing a person wore may indicate the type of weather he or she was expecting. The damages to a vehicle or skid marks in a roadway will help an investigator determine what occurred in the wreck. The size of a bullet and the marks on it will help to identify the type of gun used. There are any other number of "things" that can provide information about a case or client. It is important to remember that there is more to investigation and fact gathering than just talking to the people involved.

Was there a video camera in the area that may have recorded actions taken by the plaintiff or defendant? If so, it will be important to obtain a copy of that video. In a sexual harassment case, it may well be important to find out if the defendant has pornographic materials at his or her home or on his or her computer. When trying to defend or pursue a stalking case, find out if the defendant has such things as a video camera, photographs or belongings of the victim, or a history of physical abuse or intimidation, and whether the defendant owns a firearm. In a construction fraud case, the types of materials or equipment actually utilized by the contractor are essential as compared to what was agreed upon.

Looking for other "things" may be important even in nonlitigious areas of law. In probate and guardianship cases, for instance, it is imperative to find out exactly what the decedent or incompetent owns and to make an inventory of all of the person's belongings and assets as well as debts. This is important also in bankruptcy and in collection cases.

Wrap-up

Who, what, when, where, why, and how? Have these questions been answered? As you move through the case, be sure to update the list of what is known and unknown. While gathering some information, you may find that there is something you forgot and you will need to add that to the list. You also might find that you need to delete something from the list. A spreadsheet or document management system will help to note the relationship between the information and facts gathered and the parties involved. As documents and information are received, update the spreadsheet or management system. Name the particular information or document, and then list the date received, the source of the information, the creation date, and so forth. Also, indicate which fact or element of the case to which the particular document or information relates, the individual(s) or party(ies) to whom it relates, and whether the information supports or controverts the fact or element. Finally, include a field for *last updated* or *last revised* date, and be sure that this date is updated each time you add information to the spreadsheet.

Following is a sample of a document list.

Document Type	Date Received	Source	Creation Date	Author	Recipient	Related Fact	Related Element
Last updated 2/19/08							
Letter	2/15/08	Client (Company A)	2/10/07	Alex Alexander, CPA of Company B	John Doe, Company A CEO	Payment will not be made	Breach of contract
Internal memo	1/25/08	Company B	1/28/07	Joe Smith, Company B CEO	Alex Alexander, Company B CPA	Instructions to withhold payment to Company A	Breach of contract
Internal memo	2/15/08	Client	2/15/07	John Doe, Company A CEO	Employees of Company A	Services to Company B are discontinued	Breach of contract
Inspection report	1/25/08	Company B	1/25/07	Engineering USA, Inc.	Joe Smith, Company B CEO	Company A services are not up to par	Failure to perform

Keep the supervising attorney advised as you gain information about the case. He or she is your guide and can help to determine if there is something that is missing from the investigation or whether a particular track should not be pursued. The more you work with an attorney, the quicker you will come to know the information that attorney believes is important to the types of cases and area of law in which he or she practices. Be sure to note the bad along with the good. Rarely is one side or the other completely "good" or "bad," and the attorney needs to know it all so that any issues can be addressed with the client as they come up.

Be flexible, because some facts will be in controversy and may remain in controversy despite your best efforts to determine "the truth." A paralegal's responsibility is to obtain information, but in so doing, it is not always possible to find the answers to everything. As you become more experienced, you will find that many of the actions taken in investigation become second nature. In addition, curiosity and common sense are essential characteristics of a good investigator and a good paralegal.

Once again, before speaking with anyone, *always* identify yourself, the attorney for whom you work, and the client you represent. A paralegal is ethically obligated to ensure that anyone with whom he or she comes into contact understands that the paralegal is *not* an attorney, cannot give legal advice, and is not licensed to practice law. Consequently, it is essential to always be honest. Never mislead someone in the zeal to obtain information from that person, no matter how well intentioned you may be.

Trial Presentation Software

There are several trial presentation software programs available. These programs provide a vehicle for creating presentations that can include such things as audio, video, digital photographs, and charts and graphs for use at mediation, hearings, and trial. Take time to thoroughly review the needs of your client and the client's case in order to determine which program should be utilized. Another determining factor will be who actually will run the presentation at mediation or trial—and whoever that is must be thoroughly trained on the program.

Prior to trial, contact the court and request the opportunity to review the courtroom and make a dry run of the presentation using the same equipment and software that will be used at trial. Always have spare bulbs, batteries, power cords, and so forth available in the event of a malfunction, and always have a backup plan in the event the equipment fails completely. The backup plan should include hard copies of demonstrative evidence that can be given to the jury in place of the trial presentation.

Chapter 3

Document Management

T HE EFFECTIVE AND EFFICIENT organization and management of documents transcends all areas of practice and is of prime importance. Whether it is a case with only a few documents or a case with many boxes of documents, it is vital to be able to locate a specific document or piece of information when you need it. This is a major area of responsibility assigned to paralegals.

BASIC FILE MANAGEMENT

Even in the most simple of cases, it is important to have a system that allows you to locate documents quickly and efficiently. This may be as straightforward as file folders that are clearly labeled. The description on the label must be one that can be easily recognized by anyone accessing the file. Some offices have standardized methods of labeling files and subfiles, combining a numbering system along with a descriptive term. If you do not have such a system, one way to organize files is to set up subfiles as follows: Correspondence; Attorney Notes; Memos; Pleadings; Court Orders; Discovery Requests (be specific, such as Interrogatories to Defendant X); Discovery Responses (be specific); Depositions (identified by deponent); Employment Agreement; Billings and Advanced Expenses. It may be necessary to add additional files by year or volume number as the case progresses; for example, Correspondence — 2007, or Correspondence — Volume 2. You might want or need to create an index of some of the files. This is especially helpful with pleadings, motions, and other court documents, as well as discovery. The index will help you to see, at a glance, what was filed, when, and by whom.

Typically, files are arranged in folders in reverse chronological order, oldest at the bottom to newest on top. If you are organizing documents into notebooks, arrange them in chronological order, oldest in the front to newest at the back.

Depositions are usually arranged alphabetically by the last name of the deponent. In complex cases, you might arrange the depositions by issue or in order of testimony.

COMPUTER FILE ORGANIZATION

An effective document management system should include organization of computer files. Set up folders much as you would a paper file, with subfolders and files. It is then a simple matter to click on the appropriate folder and locate a specific document or piece of information. You can refine or expand your system as the case requires. As the case progresses, you will likely add sections for depositions and other discovery, trial preparation, and perhaps post-trial matters.

You will receive a great deal of information electronically, and it will be necessary to integrate it into your organizational system. For example, depositions will be provided on disc or by email and should be maintained in computer files as well as in a paper file.

Some jurisdictions now require that discovery be provided electronically. The requests and responses must be organized and maintained.

Many courts require electronic filing. Check with the appropriate jurisdiction for their requirements. Develop a system that will allow you to add electronic signatures and that will provide easy identification of documents that have been filed electronically. This might be as simple as including a notation in the name of the document.

You may be required to provide certain documents electronically even in jurisdictions that do not have electronic filing. For example, as you near trial, you may have to provide jury instructions to the court on disc or by email. Know the requirements and preferences of the court and staff. Your system should easily identify what has been provided to whom.

DEVELOPING A SYSTEM

Develop a system that works for you and the attorney or team assigned to the case. Control is key. It is important for the paralegal to be involved in the management of the documents from the beginning of the case. It is easier to manage the documents from the start rather than try to catch up once the case is well under way. It is very important that the documents be managed and maintained throughout the course of the case. They should be incorporated into your system as they are received. There may be occasions when you are brought in in the middle of the case to manage the documents, however, many of the same principles will apply.

Whether the case is simple or complex, the goal is the same. Keep it simple. Do not make it more difficult than it needs to be. The goal is to locate things as needed. As cases become more complex, it becomes more important to have a plan in place. Meet with the team early on in the process. Everyone should have input into the organization and management of the information. It is also important to understand the responsibilities of each team member and support staff. Who is doing what and when? Everyone on the team should understand the issues in the case. Everyone should be aware of deadlines. Try to get some sense of the quantity of documents involved. Is it one box or one room full of boxes? Determine your storage needs. Where are the documents located? Will it be necessary for you and/ or the team to be off-site for extended periods of time? Can the project be managed in-house or will it be necessary to use an outside vendor? What types of documents must be managed and what is their condition? Are there odd or oversized documents? Are they two-sided? Are there multiple pages that are clipped or stapled? Are they originals or copies? All these things must be considered in determining the most efficient and cost-effective way to manage documents.

Documents will be gathered or produced throughout the course of the case, from the initial meeting with the client through the trial or other disposition of the case, and they must be incorporated into your system. As the amount of documents grows from 100 to 1,000 or even 100,000 or more, it will become increasingly difficult to locate items if a system has not been implemented and maintained.

Once you have a good idea of the amount and types of documents, next you will need to analyze your technology needs. Do you have the hardware and software you need to manage this project? Will you need to purchase new hardware or software? Will you need an outside vendor to copy, number, or code the documents? Again, planning is the key to the successful management of your project.

It is important that you maintain a control set of documents. If the client does not object to numbering the originals, they should be the control set. If it is necessary to copy the originals before numbering, the copies will be the control set. In this instance, you will also need a system for relating the numbered copy back to the unnumbered original. You might create a comprehensive index of all the documents, noting the location within the original control set. This might be a box number or a subfile within a box, along with the box number.

MAINTAINING THE SYSTEM

The paralegal should have control of the documents and the maintenance of the system. Originals should only be removed from the file for copying and should be immediately returned to their proper place. A working copy of the documents, or key documents, may be made for day-to-day use. This will prevent misplacement or inadvertent marking of the documents. If it is necessary to remove a document, the place should be marked (colored paper or cards are helpful), noting what was taken and by whom and when they were removed. The paralegal should be diligent in ensuring that this procedure is followed by everyone accessing the file. The more people working on the file, the easier it is to misplace documents or to disrupt the organization of the file.

Review the documents as they are received. It may be helpful to prepare a summary of the documents, noting pertinent information. For example, if the document references a key meeting, that should be noted. You may choose to revise the summary at a later time, refining it or adding more detail as appropriate. Organize your documents before you start numbering. Determine the relevancy of each document and if the documents are privileged or attorney work product. These documents should be maintained separately or clearly marked as privileged so they are not inadvertently produced. It will be helpful to note why they should not be produced (e.g., privileged, not responsive).

When you receive documents from an adverse party, tag key documents and note them on your index. Many of the documents may not be relevant. It will be helpful to create a file of these key documents, being careful to maintain the originals as they were received and noting the pertinent information on your index and summary. If the documents were not numbered by the party producing them, you should do so, identifying the producing party.

NUMBERING DOCUMENTS

Numbering each piece of paper is commonly referred to as "Bates numbering." You might still use the Bates numbering stamp, which stamps consecutive numbers on pages, but there are newer and more efficient ways of applying the numbers. You can create your own labels to apply to each page using numbering software. In addition, there is software available for copy machines that will number the documents as they are copied. You can also opt to use a vendor who has the technology to number the documents. If the case is large or complex, you might add letters before the numbers to identify the parties producing the documents; for example, the defendants may be identified by X, Y, or Z or the first two or three letters of their last name. This will allow you to tell at a glance which party produced the document. Keep in mind that you must maintain the numbering system. As documents are gathered, they should be numbered consecutively, starting from the end of the previously numbered set. Numbering should be done before the documents are copied so that all sets will have the same numbers.

INDEXING DOCUMENTS

Indexing the documents is vital to locating and tracking documents coming in and going out. Work with the attorney and other members of the team to develop the information to be tracked in the index. It is important to have enough information to allow you to do an effective computer search of the index. The size or complexity of the case will dictate the level of detail needed in the index. You will want enough flexibility to allow you to sort the information in a useful manner. For example, the table below could be sorted to list all the documents received from Defendant X in response to a Request for Production of Documents.

A simple table or spreadsheet is a good place to start.

Bates Numbers	Source	Date Produced	Produced By	Description	Reviewed By
AA 0001 – AA 0025	Client	06/23/06	Client	Contract w/ Def. X	Atty. A
XX 0025 – XX 0132	Response to RFP	12/12/06	Def. X	Spreadsheets	
BA 0001 – BA 0346	Third party subpoena	8/1/06	Bank BA	Statements	Atty. B

Your index might be as basic as this example, or it might be highly detailed depending upon the type or complexity of the case or the documents being indexed. Keep in mind that a document may consist of several pages, and it is important to note the range of those pages in the index. This allows you to reference one specific page of a document if necessary. It is also important to note the source of the document so you will know where you obtained the document.

You should index all documents produced to you by your client, your adversaries, and from other sources, such as nonparties. You should also index, in the same manner, documents you produce to your adversaries. Not only will this be a record for you of what has been produced, but you will know if a response needs to be supplemented at a later date. You should create a separate index for each category of documents. While this is a time-consuming task it will reap great rewards in the time and energy saved in being able to locate documents through the course of the case.

CREATING A DATABASE

You might choose to create a more sophisticated database to index your documents. A database is a collection of specific, structured information. One example of a common database is a telephone directory. Each entry or record is structured the same way. In this example, the database is organized by the person's last name, then first name, address, and telephone number. It is typically organized alphabetically, but the database is structured so that it could be sorted differently if necessary. For example, it might be desirable to sort the information by the telephone number prefix.

Much of the same information is used throughout the life of the case. The database, or group of records, should contain uniform sets of specific information (or fields) that can be searched, sorted, listed, and reported in a number of ways.

You might also wish to scan and code some or all of the documents as a part of the management process. As discussed earlier, you should have analyzed your technology needs and determined if this will be done in-house or by an outside vendor.

If the project will be handled in-house, you might use a database program that is readily available with most office software that can be adapted to suit your needs, or you may choose to purchase a program that is specifically designed for law-related use. The larger the project, the more likely it is that you will need a program that is designed to handle the demand. Consideration should be given to the existing need, the initial cost, the versatility of the program and its compatibility with existing programs, the time it will take to install and implement the program, training, and the personnel needed to implement and maintain the program. Keep in mind the time you have to complete the project as you decide whether to handle the project in-house or use an outside vendor. It can take a great deal of time from the start to the finish of the project.

HARDWARE AND SOFTWARE

Whether you are considering purchasing software and hardware or using an outside vendor, do your homework. Research the history and the track record of the product or the vendor. Meet with the vendor. Ask for samples and demonstrations of the product or previous projects. Ask for references and talk to others who have used the product or vendor. The vendor needs to have experience in handling this type and scope of project. What type of quality control will be used? Will there be a guarantee? How will your documents be maintained securely? Determine the training and support system that will be available to you. It will do you little good to have an expensive, complex system that no one can use. Likewise, if a vendor has completed the project, you or someone on the team will need to be trained and have support in using the system. Remember, the goal is to be able to quickly and efficiently locate documents; if you cannot do that, the system is of little use to you.

IMAGING DOCUMENTS

Document imaging can reduce the amount of paper that must be managed and kept immediately available. Once the documents have been scanned and coded (entered into a database), they can be stored in a less accessible area. But, like all systems, for this to be functional, it must be planned carefully and maintained and kept up-to-date through the life of the case.

As with other systems, a great deal of thought and planning should precede the implementation of the project. The database is the key to the system and should contain sufficient information to allow you to adequately identify documents, but it should not be so massive that it will be difficult to search. Much like the index discussed earlier, the database should contain the Bates number range, the date of the document, the type of document, the author, the source, a brief description, and the issue to which the document relates. The database also should have fields for the identity of the person entering the data and the date it was entered. This will help with quality control. The people creating the database must be consistent in entering the data. This is the key to the entire project. If abbreviations are used, they must be used consistently. It is helpful if the database has drop-down boxes giving the appropriate selections rather than leaving the choice to the person entering the data. Formulas should be created so that all dates and numbers are entered in the same way. Other fields might prompt with a question that requires a yes or no response. This ensures consistency and functionality of the system. You will have to be able to retrieve the documents, so training will be necessary for both those entering the data and those who will ultimately use the system.

Quality control is essential. Start with a control group of documents to see how the documents scan. They must be legible or they are of little use. The database must be functional. Do a trial run with the control group. By testing early in the process, you can more easily make adjustments than you can once the amount of documents has grown in size. You should continue to check the quality of the scanning and the database throughout the process. The team should meet regularly to be kept advised of the status of the project and to troubleshoot any potential problems. Every member of the team and those who support them should be able to retrieve documents as they are needed.

PRIVILEGED VERSUS NON-PRIVILEGED DOCUMENTS

When reviewing your documents, you must determine if the document falls into the privileged category, in whole or in part.

Attorney/client privilege is the legal doctrine that prohibits an attorney who represents a client from testifying in open court and revealing the secrets of the client.

Some types of documents that might be subject to attorney/client privilege are communications from the client to the attorney, such as letters, telephone messages, memos, and emails; the same types of communications from the attorney to the client, including drafts; transcripts or records of conversations between the client and attorney; and certain documents created within the business structure if the client is a corporation. This is by no means an exhaustive list but a basic guideline. The attorney should provide specific guidelines for you for each case.

The work-product doctrine is different from, and broader than, the attorney/client privilege. This doctrine protects any materials prepared by the attorney and the paralegal, whether or not the material has been provided to the client. Some consultants or experts hired by the attorney during the litigation may also be covered by this doctrine. However, this rule may not extend to reports prepared by the expert. This should be determined by the attorney. The purpose of this doctrine is to protect the thoughts and mental impressions of the attorney, including opinions, strategy, legal theories, and analysis of facts and issues pertaining to the case. In claiming work-product privilege, the attorney must show that the material was prepared in anticipation of litigation or for trial. Some types of documents that may be protected by the work-product privilege are attorney memos; notes or emails to the file or other attorneys or paralegals regarding strategy, issues, theories, or status of the case; and attorney notes relating to materials prepared for trial, such as notes of conversations with witnesses or outlines of testimony or parts of the trial. This list is not meant to be all-inclusive and the attorney should make the final determination in each case. As a means of precaution, when such materials are created, they can be marked "Confidential — Attorney Work Product."

Sometimes only a part of a document is privileged. For example, if an attorney makes notes on a document that is not otherwise privileged, only the attorney's notes are privileged, and they may be redacted if the document is to be produced. Proper redaction is very important but can be a tedious and time-consuming task. There are several ways to redact documents. It is very important to maintain the original document. A copy should be made before the redaction. The words or areas to be redacted can be covered with a white tape made for that purpose or a liquid product, or they can be blacked out. (You should be aware that the words sometimes show through the blacking out, so a copy must be made of the blacked out pages before producing.) The document or the redacted areas should be marked "redacted" so that it is clear that this has been done. The attorney should direct you on what to redact and how to mark the redactions.

When documents or information is not produced by claiming the attorney/client or work-product privilege, the party claiming the privilege must provide a description of the documents or information not produced without revealing any of the privileged information. A privilege log should be created for this purpose and should also include the redacted documents. An example of a privilege log can be found in chapter 4, Discovery.

In some instances, it may be necessary to request a Protective Order from the court. This may be required when the client is asked to produce documents or things that may be proprietary in nature or contain trade secrets, research, product development, or customer information.

USING BINDERS FOR ORGANIZATION

You may prefer to organize some types of documents in three-ring binders. This can be especially helpful in organizing responses to discovery requests with an appropriate index with important issues and key documents noted and marked. You might have a notebook for each party's responses, or you might need multiple notebooks in larger cases. Each volume should be marked clearly and noted appropriately on the index. This is also a good way to organize and index pleadings.

Other cases might have a large number of medical records. These might be organized by subfile for each health care provider or in notebooks tabbed by provider. You might choose to organize a set of the records chronologically. As you review the records, create a simple chart or index of the medical treatment in chronological order, noting dates and providers of treatment, with a brief summary of each record. Mark and note those records that contain key information.

Depositions can be organized in the same way, with the exhibits tabbed by number. The attorney may create, or ask you to create, a summary of the deposition that should be kept with the deposition. Most depositions are now provided electronically. There are software programs available that have search capabilities. If you have done searches or queries for particular issues, words, or phrases, print a copy of that report to keep with the deposition. Most depositions, whether in hard copy or electronic format, have a word index showing the page and line for all the words in the deposition. Some attorneys prefer to work with the hard copy while others prefer the electronic version. Be sure to maintain the original deposition. Make a working copy if the attorney wants to make notes on or mark the deposition.

You may want or need to create one or more issue files containing all the pertinent documents pertaining to a specific issue. You can do the same thing with "hot" documents, whether they are the key documents to prove your case, disprove your opponent's case, or impeach or rebut the testimony of a party or witness. The same documents should also be located in the file pertaining to that party or witness. You should have a similar file for documents that will be used as exhibits at depositions or trial.

MANAGING TRIAL DOCUMENTS

It is important to discuss the management of documents for trial. As you get closer to trial, you will already have implemented a system for managing the majority of the documents, but there will be additional organization and preparation for trial. You will be creating trial notebooks or files, as the attorney prefers, incorporating some of the work you have already completed. In doing so, the below guidelines should be followed:

- It may not be necessary to include all the motions and orders filed in the case in the trial materials. You need to include the Complaint and Answer, and any Cross-Complaints and Counterclaims. You also need to include all dispositive motions, such as Motions for Summary Judgment and all supporting materials and corresponding orders. The following should also be included: Motions to Quash or Strike certain evidence; Motions in Limine, or other pretrial motions. All pertinent materials and supporting research should be included with these motions. Include any orders from the court pertaining to the trial as well as all the witness and exhibit lists that have been filed. Separate and tab each section.

- You should maintain files both in hard copy and electronically of each index and summary you have created. It will be helpful to have quick and easy access to this information, especially if you are in the courtroom and need to find a specific item from a box or a database.

- You should have a file of all the subpoenas that have been issued for the trial, and a copy should be placed in each witness file.

- You should create separate files for the instructions filed by each party as well as the court, dividing them into issue or contention instructions and preliminary and final instructions.

- If a trial brief was prepared, include it in the trial materials, along with any pertinent research materials or supporting documentation.

- If there have been any stipulations of the parties, those should be a part of your trial documents.
- You should include pertinent court rules, jury rules, and rules of evidence in your materials.

Exhibits will be created from certain documents and information you have previously organized. Trial preparation and participation are discussed in greater detail in chapter 5.

CONCLUSION OF THE CASE

Once the case is concluded, all the bills and subrogated parties have been paid, all monies have been disbursed to the client, and all deadlines for appeal or other relief have passed, the documents that have been collected throughout the course of the case must be managed. Your firm likely has a procedure in place for closing and/or destroying both paper and computer files.

If the case has gone to trial, you will probably need to do some reorganization. Put things back into their proper file or location. Clean out the trial notebooks. Retain all pertinent trial materials, including notes and one copy of the trial notebook, until all the deadlines for post-trial relief have passed. Return all personal materials and items, such as photographs or birth or death certificates, to the client or their owner.

Determine your attorney's preference or policy for retaining copies of pleadings. The court will retain the complete file so you may not want or need to keep a set, though some attorneys or firms prefer to keep a complete set of the pleadings. You should organize the complete set in chronological order.

Your attorney may wish to keep certain key pleadings for future reference. You can create separate files of specific types of documents, such as trial briefs or Motions for Summary Judgment, and maintain them separately from closed or client files. You may choose to keep notebooks or file folders of sample documents. It is helpful to create and maintain an index of those documents. You may choose to do this on the computer, scanning documents not generated by your office, rather than maintaining paper files.

Saving legal research materials may be useful in preparing briefs and motions for appeal and for later issues on the same subject. If the appeal deadlines have passed, you may wish to create an index, noting the pertinent issue along with the name and number of the case for later access. If you have general research for issues, such as Motions in Limine or Motions for Summary Judgment, you may wish to create a separate index for each type of applicable research. This eliminates the need to keep the paper copies. The index should include the name and citation of the case and the main issue or subject matter.

You may want to retain other types of information for later use, such as factual research or expert research, depositions, or reports. These also should be maintained separately from the client's closed file for future reference.

PREPARING FILES FOR STORAGE

Once the files have been organized and you have retrieved anything you need to return to the client or that you want to save for future reference, clean out the file and prepare it for storage. Your firm might have a procedure in place for what is maintained in a closed file or how it is stored. Some firms store the closed files electronically by scanning everything that will be retained, while others might have off-site storage. Once you have determined the policy for what is kept, clean out the file accordingly (your attorney, however, may wish to do this). Discard any duplicates. Consolidate where you can. Make new labels if that is necessary. Just as with an open file, you want to be able to locate what you might need within a closed file. Take out partially used legal pads, retaining the used sheets. Empty notebooks, maintaining the contents as appropriate, and save them for future use. Check the files for other office supplies. Recycle what you can, including the manila folders. It is important that any confidential client information be destroyed. This is typically done by shredding and recycling all the documents.

PRACTICE-RELATED DOCUMENTS AND FILES

It is helpful to organize and maintain documents and files that you will find useful in your day-to-day practice. This can be done in hard copy, electronically, or as a combination of both. Collect and create forms and samples of documents that are used frequently, such as the following: Complaints, Motions for Continuance or Extensions of Time, discovery requests, deposition question outlines, jury instructions, Motions in Limine, and court rules from different jurisdictions. It also can be helpful to have a collection of briefs, depositions, and legal research. Similar issues and types of cases may arise, and there is no need to "recreate the wheel." But always be cautious to make the documents case-specific when you are using documents previously created.

Experts are frequently used over again in litigation. It is helpful to retain expert witness materials and files upon the close of a case. Include the expert's curriculum vitae, reports, depositions, and any other pertinent information. Maintain these files and create an index in a searchable database. This will prove invaluable if it becomes necessary to retain an expert in the same type of case. Many professional organizations also keep banks of these materials that you can access or copy.

Chapter 4
Discovery

BLACK'S LAW DICTIONARY, SIXTH Edition, defines and describes discovery as follows: "The pre-trial devices that can be used by one party to obtain facts and information about the case from the other party in order to assist the party's preparation for trial. Under Federal Rules of Civil Procedure (and in states which have adopted rules patterned on such) tools of discovery include: depositions upon oral and written questions, written Interrogatories, production of documents and things, permission to enter upon land or other property, physical and mental examination, and requests for admissions."

Discovery serves many purposes: to avoid prejudicial surprise, to narrow and clarify the issues, to provide parties with full knowledge of the facts, and to prevent delays at trial in the interest of judicial economy. The basic forms of discovery are Interrogatories, Requests for Production of Documents,

Requests for Admissions, and depositions. There are other forms of discovery, but these are the most commonly used.

Scope of Discovery

Check the applicable rules (federal, state, and/or local) in the jurisdiction where suit has been filed. Generally, parties may obtain discovery regarding any non-privileged matter that is relevant to the subject matter involved in the pending action, whether it relates to the claim or defense of the party seeking discovery or the claim or defense of any other party. It includes the existence, description, nature, custody, condition, and location of any books, documents, or other tangible things, and the identity and location of persons having knowledge of any discoverable matter. Also check the applicable rules regarding a duty to supplement your answers to Interrogatories.

What Is Discoverable?

You may discover any non-privileged information that is either relevant to the subject matter at hand or reasonably designed to lead to the discovery of relevant matter. Some things that might be requested include, but are certainly not limited to, factual information, such as business structure; the existence of liability insurance, including the amount; medical history; identity and location of witnesses and experts; information on prior litigation; and photographs and other physical evidence.

> Relevant matters typically are not privileged and include information that:
> - Is subject to the matter involved in the pending action
> - Is relevant to the subject matters and helps a party prepare for trial or facilitates pretrial settlement
> - Uncovers the ultimate facts behind the pleadings

Relevant information is subject to discovery even though it may be inadmissible at trial. Information may be sought concerning potential as well as actual issues in a case. Discovery may be obtained with regard to damages even before a determination of liability has been made. Information on damages has been held to be relevant because it precipitates pretrial settlement in that it allows both sides an opportunity to evaluate the financial impact of the litigation.

What Is Not Discoverable?
Privilege rules apply to all discovery devices. The most frequent privileges raised are attorney/client and work-product privileges.

All written and oral communications between attorneys and clients are privileged and not discoverable. This privilege extends to paralegals.

Paralegal work done at an attorney's direction or under an attorney's supervision qualifies for work-product privilege protection. Examples of paralegal work product include interoffice memoranda; memoranda of telephone conversations and/or interviews with clients; notes from meetings with clients in preparation of discovery responses; memoranda of document screening or site inspections; informal investigation memoranda; document production notes; factual or legal research memoranda; opening case memos; trial preparation materials; and diagrams, charts, graphs, or other demonstrative evidence. As a safeguard, it is a good practice to stamp sensitive memos "Prepared at the direction of Attorney (name)." Other types of confidential documents may not be discoverable.

Additional types of information that may not be discoverable include the following:
- Personal/confidential records
  - Lifetime medical or psychiatric history
  - Tax returns (unless particularly relevant to the litigation)
  - Financial condition of a party if there is no punitive damage claim
- Official records, such as bank statements

There may be exceptions if the information is specifically relevant to the case.

INTERROGATORIES

Interrogatories are written questions that may be served on any adverse party who has made an appearance in an action through filing a Complaint, a Cross-Complaint, or an Answer. They may not be served on nonparties. Interrogatories are specific questions that must be answered under oath and within a certain statutory time limit. They are economical discovery devices for obtaining basic information about the opposing party, the party's version of the transaction or occurrence, and the existence of items of evidence to support their version of the transaction or occurrence.

Applicable trial rules will dictate the form of the Interrogatories, but typically the answers to the Interrogatories are signed, under oath, by the person making the answers. Objections are signed by the attorney making them. The typical response time is 30 days. Federal rules as well as many local rules limit the number of Interrogatories to 25, including subparts. Additional Interrogatories may be served with leave of the court or pursuant to the agreement of the parties. In some states, trial rules do not restrict the number of Interrogatories that may be served, but case law suggests that too many may be unduly burdensome, and a Motion for Protective Order may be sought and obtained. In some jurisdictions, additional Interrogatories may be propounded only for "good cause shown and upon leave of the court."

Reasons for Using Interrogatories

There are many reasons for using Interrogatories as discovery tools. Generally, they can be used to request details and specifics of the allegations in the Complaint and Answer or other pleadings. This will be helpful in probing the merits of the opposing party's claim or defense. They are also useful for learning the extent of the other party's personal information and for identifying other persons who might have valuable information. In cases involving injury, Interrogatories can be helpful in identifying the nature and extent of injuries and also in determining any preexisting injuries or conditions.

Advantages of Interrogatories

There are advantages to using Interrogatories over other forms of discovery, such as depositions. They are economical, the only cost being the time it takes to review the file and draft them. They are fast and efficient. The other side is forced to provide you with information that may be important to developing your case. They are flexible and can be used for any number of purposes from gathering the most basic information to helping to define the issues. They complement other methods of discovery. They are frequently accompanied by Requests for Production and Requests for Admissions, which will be discussed later. Interrogatories can be used as follow-up devices after other discovery. For example, you may want to follow up on something that was discussed in a deposition, responses to earlier Interrogatories, questions regarding documents received in response to a Request for Production, or to narrow issues or defenses that were raised in a Complaint or Answer. Interrogatories are frequently used at the beginning of a lawsuit, and they are submitted along with a Complaint if an initial investigation has not provided sufficient information. The use of Interrogatories is especially helpful for getting information that was not provided informally, such as the existence and amount of insurance coverage.

Disadvantages of Interrogatories

There are some disadvantages to using Interrogatories. They can be directed only to parties. They are slow. There are frequent delays and requests for additional time within which to respond. The party's responses will be carefully crafted. There is no spontaneity such as there would be in a deposition. There is no chance for follow-up questions as there would be in a deposition. There is no chance to size up an adversary or a client's credibility or witness potential.

Preparing to Draft Interrogatories

You should have, or should begin, a collection of standard Interrogatories for different types of cases. You can then tailor them to make them case-specific. If you see some questions you like on a set of Interrogatories that you are answering, save them for future reference. Be very careful to make them case-specific. Before you begin, you should know the case on which you are working inside and out. Read all the pleadings, the client intake memo, relevant contracts and other documents, incident reports, and any other relevant material. Many ideas for questions will come from this information. It is also necessary to know the legal issues of the case to ask about the facts upon which those issues are based.

Determine what you know. Once you have learned the issues, match them with the facts you know from your client's point of view and with the facts you have learned through investigation or informal discovery.

Determine what you need to know and the areas about which you need more information. Frame your questions along the investigative questions who, what, where, why, when, and how, as shown below:
- Who are you?
- Where were you and when?
- Why were you there?
- What happened? What did you do?
- How did the incident occur?

Consider asking your questions in such a way that the story of the facts comes out chronologically. By doing this, you develop a factual basis in a chronological sequence of events, which is the most accurate method of presenting a case story. Use simple words and short sentences whenever possible. Avoid questions that call for simple yes or no answers, unless you are able to immediately follow up those questions.

Phrase Interrogatories so the person answering them will have to indicate whether he or she is taking them from firsthand knowledge, second-hand knowledge, or relying on documents, so that you can learn the source of critical information. Avoid poorly drafted Interrogatories that allow for incomplete or evasive answers.

Use the "ladder" approach as an effective drafting technique. Ask broad questions that would elicit a yes or no answer, then follow with specific questions relating to one or more of the possible responses. This approach is effective but uses a lot of questions, so it is usually best to avoid yes or no questions if you know, or are fairly certain of, the answer. You may certainly ask questions such as the following:

- Could you please state the date and state of the defendant's incorporation, its principal place of business, and all members of the board of directors by name, address, and telephone number? (This combines several ladder steps but would not be considered overly broad.)
- Have you ever attended defensive driver school? If the answer is yes, please explain fully and in detail.

GENERAL TOPICS

- Identity of parties, agents, employees (business and corporation information)
- Identity of witnesses
- Identity of documents and tangible objects (e.g., photographs, physical evidence). A good standard question is to ask the answering party to identify each and every document referred to or reviewed in answering the Interrogatories.
- Identity of experts, facts, and opinions
- Details and sequences of events and transactions
- Damage information and the ability to pay, including insurance coverage
- Identity of the person who prepared the answers and the sources that person used
- Position on opinions and issues of fact. For example, if the defendant has alleged that the plaintiff was contributorily negligent, ask what specific conduct the defendant claims constituted the negligence.

Check your firm's or law school's library for books containing outlines and lists of questions. This is especially helpful when you encounter an unfamiliar type of case or matter. You will find suggested discovery requests pertaining to specific types of matters that you can tailor to fit the facts of your case.

Drafting Interrogatories

The format of the Interrogatories is prescribed by the applicable trial rules. Typically, the document would contain the caption of the case and the title of the document. There is usually an introductory paragraph citing the applicable trial rule and specifying the time within which the party must respond.

You may choose to have a definitions section. Terms used repeatedly in the Interrogatories can be defined, which would make the Interrogatories easier to follow and would effectively deter evasive answers. The definition might be as simple as a case-specific definition of the collision or the contract, or might include several pages of definitions of everything from the word "document" to the word "you." An example of this would be as follows: "Incident" or "subject incident" refers to the collision that occurred on January 22, 2006. Some states prohibit the use of introductory paragraphs or definitions. If a definition is needed, it must be set forth in the first Interrogatory within the context of the question.

Interrogatories should not be too vague, too broad, or overly exclusive. The Interrogatory should be open to one interpretation only—the interpretation of the drafting party.

Interrogatories and their responses may be introduced at trial in the same fashion that depositions are admissible. Questions should be worded in simple, nonlegal terms so that they can be understood by a jury when they are read aloud.

Remember what you learned in high-school English pertaining to sentence structure, grammar, and verb tense. Use the present tense to determine facts that are still current. Use the past tense to determine events that are over. If your question relates to both past and present events, it is best to break the question down into several questions to avoid the objection of ambiguity. If your question contains vague and ambiguous words, it is certain to be objectionable.

Draft your Interrogatories to elicit as much information as possible, but don't draft fishing expedition questions. You should limit the parameters of time and/or definition to the information sought to avoid the objection of being overly broad or ambiguous.

You must be very careful in drafting Interrogatories to imply fault. Requests for Admissions lend themselves more easily to asking a question that will imply fault on the other side; however, carefully drafted Interrogatories may reveal fault by omission and/or failure to act.

Refer to the applicable rules for the requirements of both the requesting and responding parties. An affirmation or oath of the responding party may be required. You may be required to allow sufficient space for answers. Electronic submission of the requests to the opposing party may be required. Most jurisdictions require a statement noting the date and method of submitting the requests. Some jurisdictions require that the requests be submitted to the court. Others may require just a notice to the court that the requests have been sent. Some jurisdictions might have no such requirements.

Note the date on which the response to the Interrogatories is due. It may be necessary to request that the court compel the other party to respond.

Responding to Interrogatories

Responding to Interrogatories requires a substantial amount of work. A large part of the information necessary to prepare the answers must be obtained quickly from the client. Promptly send a copy of the Interrogatories to the client, explaining the discovery process to the client if you have not already done so. Explain that the client has a duty to answer, that the opposing counsel has the right to gather information that may lead to the admissibility of discoverable evidence, and the consequences of not answering. Ask the client to read them carefully and to begin to pencil in the answers. Assure the client that they are not as bad as they look and that you will work on them together. Highlight the questions that you need the client to answer specifically. You may choose to skip this step and just meet directly to gather information. Give a specific date by which to respond to you rather than just telling the client 10 days or 30 days. Follow up with a reminder if necessary.

Clients may have different reactions to beginning the discovery process. Some are puzzled, others are reluctant, some are resentful, and some just refuse to answer without coaxing. Frequently, by the time the client has sought the services of an attorney, there is a lot of animosity toward the opposing party and/or insurance company. Clients are usually much more receptive to the process when they are assured that you will be submitting the same types of questions to the opposition. It is also helpful to tell the client that by taking the necessary steps to gather the information and to provide thorough and complete answers to these Interrogatories, you are also preparing for the client's deposition and later testimony.

Calendar the date the responses are due, and read the questions carefully. Also review the definitions section. Review the file and all information provided by the client, and begin to draft the answers. Know your attorney's style and approach to answering Interrogatories and making objections.

Use tight, precise language, giving the information that has been requested. The responses should state just the facts without amplification. However, you might take this opportunity to expand the answer to questions involving injuries or other damages and the ramifications of those injuries or damages. It is a matter of style, but you may prefer to answer the questions in a narrative form rather than a list answering each subpart separately.

Answer all the questions. If an Interrogatory is not objected to, it must be answered. Check the applicable rules to see if each objection must be signed by the attorney. This is generally done immediately following the objection. Objections will be discussed in the next section.

If you do not have an answer, you may respond that you do not have the information or that the information will be supplied later. For example, if you are asked early on in the investigation process to name the witnesses who will testify at trial, you may answer that it has not yet been determined and will be supplied when the information becomes available. (Of course, you then have a duty to provide that information upon its availability.) You may also answer that investigation and discovery are ongoing and you reserve the right to supplement an answer.

If the question calls for a particularly long answer, you may make a list (if appropriate) and attach it separately. If you have not done so before now, this is a good opportunity to organize your file, summarize all medical or other bills and damages, and make lists of all health care providers or other items pertinent to your case. It is then an easy matter to keep these lists updated if expenses are ongoing.

After drafting the answers, return them to the attorney for review, noting specifically if there are any questions that the attorney needs to answer.

Return the completed Interrogatories to the client for the client's review and any necessary corrections. The Interrogatories must be signed by the person answering, not the attorney.

Objections to Interrogatories

An Interrogatory not objected to must be answered. The specific grounds for the objection must be set forth in the response. If the question is objectionable, no response is required, but you should still state an objection. Depending on the situation, it may not be permissible or advisable to respond to the Interrogatory with the single word "Objection."

The major grounds for objecting to Interrogatories include the following:

- *Basic relevance.* The standard for relevancy is quite broad; therefore, the courts generally do not look favorably upon this objection. The objection may be made that the information sought is not calculated to lead to the discovery of admissible evidence.
- *Broad and remote.* The question is overly broad without a limiting time factor and deals with issues remote in time.
- *Right of privacy.* Matters of a sensitive, confidential nature (e.g., entire history of medical records, financial information, tax returns, drug and alcohol rehabilitation treatment) may be objectionable, depending upon the facts and circumstances of the case.
- *Unduly burdensome.* This objection is frequently used when information sought is a matter of public record or when it is easily or more readily obtained by the opposing party.
- *Argumentative.* The form of the question is argumentative.
- *Uncertain, ambiguous, unintelligible.* The responding party is under no duty to rewrite and then answer a poorly drafted Interrogatory or to speculate as to the meaning or intent of the propounding party.
- *Continuing Interrogatories.* Interrogatories requiring a continuing duty upon the responding party to supplement an answer are typically not allowed. Check the applicable trial rules.
- *Asked and answered.* It is not enough to respond "asked and answered," you must identify specifically when the question was previously asked and answered and restate the answer.

It is not grounds for objection that the information sought will be inadmissible at the trial if the information sought appears reasonably calculated to lead to the discovery of admissible evidence.

Supplementing and Amending Responses

Depending upon the pertinent rules, a party who has responded to a Request for Discovery with a response that was complete when made may be under no duty to supplement except in the following three cases:

1. A party is under a duty to supplement responses with respect to any question directly addressed to:
   a. The identity and location of persons having knowledge of discoverable matters
   b. The identity of each person expected to be called as an expert witness at trial, the subject matter and substance of the party's testimony
2. A party is under a duty to amend a prior response if the party obtains information upon the basis of which:
   a. The party knows that the response was incorrect when made
   b. The party knows the response, though correct when made, is no longer true, and the circumstances are such that a failure to amend the response is in substance a knowing concealment
3. A duty to supplement responses may be imposed by order of the court, agreement of the parties, or at any time prior to trial through new requests for supplementation of prior responses.

REQUESTS FOR PRODUCTION OF DOCUMENTS

Within the scope of the applicable trial rules, any party can serve on any other party a request to produce, or permit to inspect and copy, any designated documents or tangible things. They may also request testing or sampling.

The request shall set forth the items to be produced or inspected either by individual item or by category, and each item or category must be described with reasonable particularity. The request should specify a reasonable time, place, and manner of making the production or inspection. As with responding to Interrogatories, any reasons for objection should be stated.

The party producing documents must produce them as they are kept in the usual course of business or organize and label them to correspond with the categories in the request.

Unlike Interrogatories, Requests for Production can be made to non-parties pursuant to applicable trial rules.

Preparing to Draft Requests for Production

Review the files, pleadings, correspondence, and documents you have received from your client.

Talk to the client. The client may know of the existence of key documents or may be able to provide you with the information necessary to describe specific documents by title or date.

Review pleadings and motions, depositions, Interrogatory responses, and other discovery as a means of learning of the existence of documents. Pay particular attention to documents that reference enclosures or attachments, and request not only the specific document but also the enclosures or attachments. If a contract and/or agreement has been mentioned, ask for not only the original but all drafts and revisions of the document.

Drafting Requests to Produce Documents

Follow the same suggestions in the section on drafting Interrogatories as you prepare to draft Requests for Production. Draft the document requests with enough specifics to avoid allowing the other side to withhold some documents, while allowing enough scope to make certain that no existing documents escape the confines of the request.

Two different drafting techniques may be used to make the requests all-encompassing and prevent the opposing party from giving incomplete or evasive responses:

1. Draft requests seeking both specifically designated items and generally described items.
2. Use specific definitions of categories and titles of specific documents, if known.

The requests must specify a reasonable date, time, and place for the production. Requests must define and designate documents sought with "reasonable particularity." You can never be sure that your request meets that standard; therefore, common sense must govern. Materials should be described by the subject matter they contain, by particular classification, or by definite time periods. Case law has held that if the request is drafted in such a manner as to allow a person of ordinary intelligence to say "I know what you want," you have met the standard of "reasonable particularity."

The following will help you to avoid objection and elicit a complete response:

- Be specific and describe the document by identifying its type (letter, agreement, contract, etc.), title, date, author, and addressee, if you know it.
- Describe the documents by specific legal theories (e.g., all correspondence, communications, memoranda, documents, and other tangible evidence pertaining to the alleged contract referred to in paragraph 3 of the Complaint).
- Set forth each category of documents separately.
- Set forth a relevant time period in the introductory paragraphs that accompany the requests.
- Request documents in all categories that are important to proving the allegations of your Complaint. It is important that privileged documents be requested, forcing your opponent to identify every document that exists in a specific category, even those that are privileged.
- Direct requests to all categories in which documents may exist. They should be broad-based and all-encompassing. Do not draft requests that are subject to objection and are merely fishing for documents. Responses that indicate that "no documents exist" are useful. It will be difficult for the party to suddenly discover documents in that category and seek to introduce them as evidence at time of trial.
- Request a realistic number of documents. Don't ask for more than you can use or handle. Only a very small percent of

documents produced are useful in discovery and trial preparation. If requests are carefully drafted based on information revealed in discovery, you can tailor document requests to specific items.

- Request each and every document that was relied on in preparation of Interrogatory responses and other discovery responses.
- Ask for documents by referring to the other party's pleadings (e.g., all correspondence, communications, memoranda, documents, and other tangible evidence that refers to, relates to, or pertains to the defendant's contentions in specific paragraphs in plaintiff's Complaint).
- Request minutes and agenda of meetings and any notes or memoranda reflecting discussions that occurred at the meeting.
- If a reference is made to telephone calls, ask for such items as the telephone logs, diaries, and appointment books.
- Ask for all materials that have been mentioned in discovery responses that are relevant to the issues of the action.

Include requests for all of the above information that may be in electronic format, including emails.

Responding to Requests for Production of Documents

Typically, the responding party has 30 days within which to respond to a Request for Production unless a motion for extension of time has been granted or the parties have agreed to a different date.

A demand for production or inspection of documents requires a specific written response to each demand or category of items stating the following:

- That the items are attached or that the responding party will comply with all the specifics of the particular demand for inspection and production
- That the responding party lacks the ability to comply with the demand. Specific reasons should be stated, demonstrating that the responding party has made a due and diligent search for the requested items and why the party is unable to comply.

Read the requests carefully. Check the requests for drafting errors. Are they too broad or vague? Do the requests seek documents in different time frames or different categories, making them objectionable? Can the opposition obtain the documents requested from sources other than your client? (Are they equally available by subpoena to a third party, etc.?) Check the requests for those items that are not in dispute, and arrange for production of those documents.

Send the requests to your client as soon as they are received. The client must make a due and diligent search for the requested items and must produce not only those documents that are under the client's direct custody and control, but also those under the control of the client's agents, employees, and the like.

Your client may already have provided you with many of the items included in the request and may mistakenly assume that they do not have a duty to look for any other documents.

In some cases, you may have to review many boxes of documents. You may be asked to identify privileged documents or to redact parts of documents if parts of the documents are not discoverable.

Each request should be carefully scrutinized so that a response can be made within the narrowest boundaries permitted by the request. Although it is not ethical to withhold documents from production if they have been properly requested, it is prudent to construe the request in the narrowest possible sense and not produce documents that have not been specifically requested.

If the requested documents merely repeat information that has been provided in prior discovery, producing them again would duplicate efforts. There is no need to provide identical documents. For example, documents that have become deposition exhibits and are later requested in a Request for Production are an example of a duplicated request that is objectionable.

All documents requested that are in the possession, custody, or control of the responding party and to which no objection is made should be produced. The documents should be produced as they are kept in the ordinary course of business or should be organized and labeled to correspond with the categories in the request. Be organized in your production of documents. Not only is this the courteous and professional way to respond, but in the long run it will help you to keep track of what has been produced, when, and to whom. Refer to chapter 3, Document Management, for additional information.

You may also object to a particular request by objecting to a specific item or category of items. Specific objections must be set forth in the same manner as they are required to be in other discovery proceedings.

You may object that the items sought are not relevant to the subject matter of the action, that they are privileged, that they are trial preparation materials, or that they are the work of an expert and do not fall within the scope of discovery permitted by the applicable trial rule. If you have documents that are responsive to the request but are privileged, you must create a privilege log to provide to the opposing party as a part of your response. While it is not necessary to produce privileged documents, you must provide a list of all privileged documents that fall within the scope of the request. A sample privilege log follows.

Date	Bates Number	Author	Recipient(s)	Description	Privilege
3/4/04	DF X-1234	John Doe	Sam Smith	Letter re: project	A/C
4/7/05	DF Y-0682	John Doe	Dave Jones	Memo re: project	W/P
5/16/05	DF X- 0589	Sam Smith	Joe Green	Fax cover sheet	A/C
11/27/05	DF Y -	Dave Jones	John Doe	Spreadsheet	W/P

REQUESTS FOR ADMISSIONS

A party may request that another party admit or deny the truth of any relevant, non-privileged matter or the genuineness of any relevant document.

Requests for Admissions differ fundamentally from other discovery tools in that they are not used to discover new information. Requests for Admissions may refer to factual matters or ultimate legal issues. Requests for Admissions often are used to narrow the issues for trial. The main advantage is that they limit the triable issues in a particular action by forcing the litigants to take fixed positions. Matters that are admitted are binding upon the responding party and may be used at trial or in Motions for Summary Judgment. Limitations are the same as limitations that apply to all forms of discovery.

The scope of Requests for Admissions is governed by the relevancy standard. They must be relevant to the issues framed by the pleadings and the subject matter of the action.

Requests for Admissions should be used to obtain admissions of facts about which there is no real dispute and should deal with singular relevant facts that can be clearly admitted or denied. They should not deal with complicated situations involving many distinct or controversial issues of fact and should not be directed to all facts of the case, but only to those that are material to proving your claims and/or defenses.

The most effective Requests for Admissions are based on the pleadings and the evidence. Depositions, Interrogatories, and Requests for Production are more appropriate discovery devices for detailed discovery.

Preparing to Draft Requests for Admissions
Requests for Admissions differ from Interrogatories in that you do not draft them based on information you need to know about your opponent's case. Rather, you base Requests for Admissions on the pleadings and relevant facts. They should be drafted in a manner that will obtain proof of your allegations, claims, or affirmative defenses.

Again, it is important to know the case you are working on inside and out. If you are drafting at the beginning of the case, draft from the pleadings. Requests for Admissions are most effective when they are based on the language of the pleadings that have been filed.

In preparing to draft requests, review the pleadings to see what has been alleged. Examine all allegations, admissions, denials, affirmative defenses, Counterclaims, and Cross-Claims, and draft your requests in language that sets forth as binding either those allegations set forth in your Complaint or those affirmative defenses set forth in your Answer. If you are further into the case, the Requests for Admissions may refer to information gathered through investigation or informal discovery, as well as information provided in response to Interrogatories and Requests for Production.

Drafting Requests for Admissions

The cardinal rule in drafting Requests for Admissions is to keep it simple. Because the purpose of Requests for Admissions is to narrow the legal and factual issues of a case, they should be narrowly drawn.

Requests for Admissions must be short and straightforward. Each request should be a simple, declarative statement rather than a question. It should address a single issue and should not be compound, complex, or ambiguous. Lengthy, complex, or compound Requests for Admissions leave the door open to qualified and unresponsive answers. Eliminate all unnecessary adjectives, adverbs, and qualifying words. Be certain you have reviewed the grammatical structure of a request. Each request should be able to stand alone and should not be vague, ambiguous, or unintelligible. The responding party is under no obligation to figure out the meaning of the requests prior to responding. An objection can be made that due to typographical and grammatical errors, the request is unintelligible. The more specific and clearly drafted the Requests for Admissions, the more difficult it is for the responding party to avoid making the admissions desired by the party making the request. The burden to be accurate and specific is on the party serving the Requests for Admissions.

Requests for Admissions should be arranged in a chronological sequence so that each admission helps you to build your case. By piling one admission on top of the other, you will put your opponent into a fixed position. As each fact is admitted, the allegations of your case will be proven and may be used at trial as evidence of binding admissions.

Requests for Admissions of the Genuineness of Documents

Requests for Admissions may be used to establish the genuineness of such documents as medical records or bills. Requests for Admissions of the Genuineness of Documents should be in the form of a declarative statement and not a question. In drafting Requests for Admissions of the Genuineness of Documents, you may combine both in the same pleading so that a reference to attached documents can be made to clear up any ambiguity that would exist without the document. There is danger, however, of referring to documents that were not authored by, or that are not within the custody of, the responding party.

Requests for Admissions as Follow-up to Other Discovery

Requests for Admissions are also useful once discovery has begun. Once you see what concessions or admissions have been made, you can draft requests to address those issues. Facts conceded in Interrogatory answers or depositions are admissions by the party but are not the same thing as conclusive binding admissions. By focusing on matters the opposition has admitted in previous discovery and drafting Requests for Admissions, you are seeking binding admissions in those areas. Matters that are admitted are deemed conclusively established for the purpose of the pending action.

Requests for Admissions of fact served after Interrogatory responses have been received are most successful when they zero in on specific Interrogatory answers relating to the liability claims. Combining Requests for Admissions with Interrogatories is effective but is no longer allowed in many states. An effective combination can be achieved by using two separate discovery documents that are served simultaneously.

Responding to Requests for Admissions

Typically, a party on whom Requests for Admissions have been served must respond, under oath, within 30 days of receiving the requests (unless an extension of time has been granted) or the matters in the request will be deemed admitted. The evidentiary effect of Requests for Admissions that are deemed admitted is that the subject matter addressed in the Requests for Admissions is no longer considered a triable issue. These admissions are treated as stipulations to the truthfulness of the matters set forth in the requests.

They are binding and conclusive to the issue, and no other evidence is necessary to establish that point at trial. Whether you intended to admit or deny the Requests for Admissions is no longer important. What is important is that by inattention, an important deadline has been allowed to expire and the result has been an automatic binding admission in favor of the propounding party. The automatic deemed admission makes Requests for Admissions a formidable weapon, because inattentiveness on the part of the responding party can have an automatic and usually devastating consequence.

Relief is possible for deemed admissions, but it is a cumbersome and costly court process. You must show good cause, demonstrating to the court the compelling reasons why you did not respond in a timely manner. It is not enough to say that someone forgot to calendar the date or that the client was on vacation.

It is crucial that you review the Requests for Admissions as soon as they arrive in your office, calendar the deadline with a reminder, and send a copy to the client.

Five Basic Responses to Requests for Admissions

There are five basic responses to Requests for Admissions:
1. You can object to the matter in the request, stating the reason for the objection.
2. You can admit the matter. You should admit whatever you do not in good faith intend to contest at trial.
3. You can deny the matter. You also may admit a part of the request and deny the second part. Your answer should be very specific to avoid confusion.
4. You can state that you cannot admit or deny, that the matter is genuinely in dispute, or even after reasonable inquiry, you do not have sufficient information to determine if the matter is true or not. You must set forth the reasons and must include a detailed description of the efforts made to obtain the information necessary to frame a response.
5. You may move for a protective order.

If you deny a Request for Admission, be certain you have substantial basis for each denial. If you deny a fact in a Request for Admission without substantial basis or knowledge and that fact is later proved at trial, the party proving the fact can receive court costs, expenses, and attorney fees. Sanctions are also allowable.

Admissions must be as complete and straightforward as the information available to the responding party permits. The responding party is also under a duty to make a reasonable inquiry to obtain the information necessary to prepare a response. An objection can be raised, however, stating that the request is ambiguous and unintelligible and can't be answered in the form that it is phrased.

Objections can be made, but they are prescribed by the applicable trial rules.

Withdrawal and Amendment of Response to Requests for Admissions

There are provisions for withdrawing and amending Requests for Admissions. The responding party who wishes to withdraw or amend an admission that was previously made must demonstrate to the court that the admission was the result of a mistake, inadvertence, or excusable neglect and that the party that obtained the admissions will not be substantially prejudiced in maintaining an action or a defense on the merits of the case by the amendment or withdrawal.

Using Requests for Admissions at Trial

Responses to Requests for Admissions may be presented to the judge or jury at the time of trial. Any matter admitted in response to a Request for Admissions, and not amended or withdrawn, is conclusively established. These admissions may be used for evidentiary purposes and laying foundation for testimony at trial. They may also be quoted verbatim by the party who has requested the admissions in support of Motions in Limine or any other motion in the action.

You may also use Requests for Admissions at trial as a basis for object-ing to evidence the other party wishes to introduce. One of the purposes of the Requests for Admissions procedure is to narrow the issues in the case. Those facts admitted through Requests for Admissions are conclu-sively established. Thus, it may be argued that a party is charged with hav-ing admitted such facts and, therefore, should not be permitted to present evidence to the contrary at trial.

There is not usually a prescribed statutory way of presenting these admis-sions. Depending on the strategy of the attorney, it may be useful to have admissions read early in the case as a means of laying the foundation for other testimony.

Requests for Admissions in Large Cases

Requests for Admissions and the Genuineness of Documents are especially useful in large cases for narrowing the focus of triable issues. For example, you may include requests to admit the genuineness of insurance policies, claim forms, inspection reports, repair invoices, photographs, and so forth. You might serve the requests along with a set of Interrogatories addressing the pleadings, the various claims and allegations made against a party, and the various affirmative defenses raised against the plaintiff.

Responding to Requests for Admissions, as well as Interrogatories and Requests for Production, in large or multiparty cases must follow a systematic approach that safeguards all deadlines, preserves the client's right to enter objections as appropriate, and provides timely and complete responses.

DEPOSITIONS

A deposition is sworn testimony given as a means of preserving testimony. Of all the means of discovery, a deposition is the only opportunity for an in-person encounter. Depositions provide attorneys an opportunity to meet and size up parties and witnesses prior to trial. Unlike most other meth-ods of discovery, depositions may be taken of both parties and nonparties. Depositions are used to gather information and facts, including testimony to be offered at trial. This is an opportunity to determine strengths and weaknesses of both sides of the case. In some instances, depositions may be taken prior to a lawsuit. The disadvantage of depositions is that they are expensive, both in out-of-pocket costs and attorney time in preparing for and taking the deposition.

As with the other forms of discovery, it is important that you become familiar with the applicable rules. Typically, one party provides a Notice of Deposition to the opposing party, stating the time and place of the deposition. Some jurisdictions may require that this be filed with the court. It will be necessary to arrange for the testimony to be recorded and transcribed. The attorney may also want a video of the deposition. You may be asked to prepare outlines or lists of questions for the attorney to use during the deposition, and you may also be asked to help your client, witness, or expert prepare for the deposition. If your client or witness has never been deposed, it is important to explain the process, such as what will happen or what might be asked. Be sure to review all documents that the client or witness might be asked to identify. Review the facts and issues. Explain that it is important to tell the truth and to listen carefully to the question and not answer until the question is complete and until the client or witness understands the question.

Discovery Depositions

Discovery depositions are the most common type of deposition. They are used to find out everything the deponent may know about the underlying facts and evidence in a case. To prepare for a deposition, you must have a full understanding of not only the underlying facts and issues but also of what already has been provided in response to other forms of discovery.

It is important to ask the deponent background questions, such as name, address, telephone number, and employment. You may need to contact that person again as you prepare for trial. You may need to do a background check of that person. One of the purposes of the deposition is to determine what kind of witness this person will make, and the attorney will want to know if there are credibility issues. The testimony in the deposition may also provide a road map to additional discovery.

You may be asked to prepare for the deposition by selecting documents that you want the deponent to identify and make a part of the deposition. You may be asked to prepare an outline of questions or areas of questions. Just as in preparing for other types of discovery, it is important that you have a complete understanding of the background of the case and what you already have in your file either from the client or what you have been provided by parties and/or nonparties in response to other discovery requests. As noted earlier, there are books available that provide outlines of questions. These are most helpful if you have never prepared for a deposition or if it is a type of case with which you are not familiar.

Evidentiary Depositions

Depositions may also be used for evidentiary purposes. This deposition can be used at trial. It is sometimes necessary to preserve the testimony of someone who is not available to testify at trial. You might consider making a video of this deposition in addition to the written transcript. This would allow the jurors to actually see and hear the witness rather than have a transcript read into the record.

Prepare for this type of deposition just as you would prepare to examine or cross-examine a witness at trial. Start with basic, identifying, and background information. Establish the deponent's familiarity with the fact situation. Establish what the witness knows from firsthand knowledge. Use the investigative questions who, what, where, why, when, and how. The questions should be tighter than in a discovery deposition. The questioning in the deposition should be just as you would want it to be in front of a jury.

If the deponent is an expert, establish the deponent's education, experience, and qualifications. Prior to the deposition, you should request a copy of the deponent's résumé or curriculum vitae, and it should be identified and made an exhibit to the deposition. If the expert witness has written articles or publications, you may want to request those also. Reviewing those writings may provide valuable information that relates to your case. It is also important to learn the expert's history of prior testimony. Many jurisdictions require that the expert provide a list that will show you not only how many times the expert has testified or been deposed but who hired the expert and if the expert testified for the plaintiff or defendant. This information will be most helpful to the attorney to explore any biases the deponent might have.

If the expert has prepared a report, that should also be an exhibit and will be used as the basis for much of the questioning. Ask the expert to explain what he or she has been asked to do, any documents reviewed, any hypotheticals used, all materials relied upon, and the conclusions reached. Follow up with questions that will explain and clarify the expert's conclusion and how that conclusion was reached. The expert should also explain any tests or experiments conducted, the basis for the test, and the results of the test. If technical terms are necessary, the deponent should define and explain each term in common language. Ask if the expert's report is a preliminary or a final report. Ask if the expert will be doing any additional work on this matter. It may be necessary to reconvene the deposition at a later date to follow up with the expert.

Objections may occur during the course of the deposition. They will be handled much as they would at trial. A basis for the objection will be stated for the record. If the deposition is used at trial, the judge will rule on the objections just as he or she would during the course of the trial. It is important that you determine how this will be done. The judge may prefer to do this prior to the presenting of the deposition. It may be necessary to have the objections or any stricken testimony removed from the video before the jury sees it.

CONCLUSION

Discovery is a vitally important part of the litigation process, whether you are submitting requests to an opponent or responding on behalf of your client. We have given a brief overview of the process. Entire books have been written on the subject. As has often been noted throughout the chapter, it is critical that the applicable court rules be determined and followed. Used correctly, discovery can be an efficient, cost-effective, and valuable tool to prove your client's case or to disprove your opponent's case. Paralegals can and should be an integral part of the discovery process.

Type of Discovery	Need Court Order?	Discovery Signed By	Under Oath?	Failure to Respond
Deposition	No	Party (if requested)	Yes	Possible sanctions
Deposition before lawsuit	Yes	Party (if requested)	Yes	Possible sanctions
Interrogatories	No	Party (lawyer signs objections)	Yes	Waive objections; possible sanctions
Requests for Admissions	No	Party or lawyer	No	Deemed admitted; possible sanctions
Request for Production of Documents	No	Lawyer	No	Waive objections; possible sanctions
Deposition on written questions	No	Party (if requested)	Yes	Possible sanctions
Motion for Physical or Mental Examination	Yes	Lawyer	No	Waive objections; possible sanctions
Request to Inspect Land	No	Lawyer	No	Waive objections; possible sanctions
FRCP 26(a)(1) disclosures	No	Lawyer	No	Possible sanctions
FRCP 26(a)(2) disclosures	No	Witness	No	Possible sanctions
FRCP 26(a)(3) disclosures	No	Lawyer	No	Possible sanctions
Nonparty Discovery				
Deposition	No, just subpoena	Witness (if requested)	Yes	Possible contempt
Deposition before lawsuit	Yes, and subpoena	Witness (if requested)	Yes	Possible contempt
Deposition on written questions	No, just subpoena	Witness (if requested)	Yes	Possible contempt
Produce documents	No, just subpoena	Witness (if requested)	No	Waive objections; possible contempt
Inspect land	No, just subpoena	Witness (if requested)	No	Waive objections; possible contempt
Deposition of witness in prison	Yes	Witness (if requested)	Yes	Possible contempt

Chapter 5

Trial Preparation and Presentation

TRIAL WORK, PERHAPS MORE than any other area of law practice, provides an excellent opportunity for paralegals to demonstrate their true value. Trial preparation ends with bringing all the elements of that preparation together in the proper order, at the right place, and at the right time. But good trial preparation is only part of the picture. Even if your trial preparation has been superior, it is of little value to the trial team unless they can pull it all together in a convincing and seemingly effortless courtroom presentation. As a paralegal member of a trial team, you become an extension of the attorney, both of you working together to ensure the best possible trial presentation. Trial attorneys can benefit from paralegal assistance in some capacity no matter the type or size of case. Trial preparation demands attention to many details and many different aspects of the case. Utilizing the skills of a paralegal frees the attorney to focus on the legal issues. In this chapter we will discuss some of the many ways in which paralegals can help the attorney prepare cases for mediation and trial, and present them successfully.

PREPARING FOR MEDIATION AND TRIAL

The key to success at mediation or trial is preparation. Managing even a simple case can be a nightmare when the case goes to trial. That is why it is essential to be well prepared. As in many aspects of life, it is the small things and details that count. Good lawyers and paralegals know that the courtroom is no place to be caught unprepared. Under the very best of circumstances, trials are very stressful. You have worked long and hard and probably waited a long time to get there. It is a very emotional time for all involved. This is the only chance you get to present your case. You want to do the very best job possible. Being organized can be the key to success. It can mean the difference between a small recovery or an outstanding verdict. Even worse, it can mean the difference between winning and losing. If you have the key document or piece of evidence that will prove the case, but cannot locate it, you have already lost.

Preparation and organization for mediation and trial should start when you first begin to work on a case. While there will be many things to do as you near the time of mediation or trial, if you have prepared the case looking toward a trial, you will be in a better position to settle the case or to have a good result at mediation. If you have gathered all of the information, interviewed all of the witnesses, gathered all of the documents, and conducted thorough discovery, you are well on your way to preparing for mediation or trial. If you have kept all of that information organized as you developed the case, and if you know what you have and how to locate it, half the battle is won.

Assemble the Trial Team

Your team might consist of an attorney and paralegal or multiple attorneys and one paralegal or more. Whatever the combination, the team should be compatible and work together comfortably. You should complement each other's strengths and compensate for each other's weaknesses. You must rely upon one another and trust that each member of the team will be working on his or her own part of the job toward a common goal. Communication is vital. Have regular meetings that should increase in frequency as the trial draws near.

Establish the Agenda

Have an initial meeting of the trial team to determine the tasks that must be accomplished. Some of the things you need to decide include motions to prepare, research that is needed, things to review, witnesses to be prepared, exhibits to be prepared, and instructions to be drafted.

Determine How Work Will Be Distributed

As each item on the agenda is being discussed, the task should be assigned to a specific team member. Each person needs to know what is expected of him or her. Consider the strengths and weaknesses of the trial team. What are the time limitations of the team members? Each person should be aware of the upcoming schedule. Who has the skill and/or inclination to accomplish specific tasks most efficiently? Who are the most and least organized? What is the experience level of each? All of this must be considered as tasks are being assigned.

Establish a Timetable

The trial team needs to know of important deadlines that must be met. Emphasize the amount of time available to complete the trial preparation tasks. At this time you also should discuss and decide on follow-up meetings.

Develop a Theme of the Case

As you gather information and begin to learn more about the case, you should begin to develop a "theme." You may not recognize it as such to begin with, but the theme frequently comes out of your early impressions. You will carry this theme through settlement negotiations, mediation, and trial.

Think toward the End as You Begin

As you work on your preliminary investigation and gathering of information, you need to give some thought to what you will need later on to prove your case. Do you need to consult an expert for advice or assistance on the preservation of evidence? Will the expert need photos, measurements, or other information that may not be available later? Do you need to preserve documents or objects that may not be available later? Are there witnesses whose testimony needs to be preserved? Should you give consideration to filing a lawsuit early on in the case to give you options to do some of these things formally?

If your client has been injured, you need to document the injuries and the effects of those injuries. You might want to take photographs or a video of the client. You might consider a "day in the life" video, if the injuries and effects are significant, that takes into account the quality of life for the injured person and his or her family, alterations made to accommodate the person's injuries, the person's lifestyle before the injury, and the person's job and how has it been affected. Hopefully, the client's condition will improve over time and a full recovery will be made, but you will have documented the struggles of having to deal with this life-altering event. This also holds true when the injured person does not survive the injuries. While time may not heal all wounds, it certainly can alter one's recollection of and reaction to events.

Develop a Settlement Brochure or Demand

At some point in the case, the attorney may want to initiate settlement discussions. You may present a thorough summary and evaluation of the entire case, from liability to damages, as a part of the settlement demand. This is the first opportunity for the opposition to learn your theories of the case and your assessment of the value of the case. You should stress the strengths of your case, keeping in mind the weaknesses. While you may not choose to share everything at this point in time, you certainly need to include enough to be helpful to your case.

Include supporting documentation that will be helpful in persuading the recipient to engage in settlement discussions. It is very important to put not only your case, but yourselves in a positive light. This may be the opposition's first impression of what they will be contending with if this matter moves to trial. You can be assured they will have checked out the reputation of your firm and the attorney of record. Now you need to give them an idea of what kind of a presentation they will see at a trial. Do your best work. Your writing should be clear and concise. Present the facts and analyze the liability. Discuss the injury or damages your client has suffered, and analyze the evaluation of those damages. Demonstrate what a jury would see and hear at trial. Your writing should be logical, organized, and letter-perfect. Your entire package should be neat and organized. It should be easy to read, with references to the location of supporting information. It is not unusual to use this initial package, with only slight alterations, later in the case as a presentation to a mediator and even later as an outline for trial presentation.

MEDIATION

The paralegal's role at mediation is just as important and can be just as crucial as at trial. Prepare for the mediation just as if it were the trial. You should be just as prepared and organized as if you were going to court. Review the file and reorganize it if necessary. You should be able to locate information in the file as needed or requested.

This will be your opportunity to present your case, not only for the benefit of the mediator, but for your opponent. Give them an idea of what they can expect to see and hear at trial. You may choose to supply them with a copy of the materials provided to the mediator. Be prepared to provide them with updates or additional information if appropriate.

Consider whether the client and/or family will take an active role in the mediation. This may be their only "day in court," and they are sometimes powerful witnesses. Do you have other witnesses who might be helpful? Consider doing a videotaped interview or clips of several short interviews. You might want to use parts of depositions. Consider highlighting not only the strengths of your case, but weaknesses in your opponent's case. There might be, for example, a witness who is very damaging to their case. Demonstrate the strength of your witnesses.

Create exhibits. Consider the size of the room and the space available to you. Make the exhibits large enough to be easily seen. Show them what a jury will see. Be creative and inventive. Determine the important elements of your case and how you can demonstrate them visually with a photograph, drawing, chart or graph, model, or perhaps a phrase excerpted from a deposition or report. You may choose to create a PowerPoint slide show using all of these elements. If the mediation does not reach a successful conclusion, you will have a head start on trial preparation.

Consider having a preliminary report from your expert. Weigh the advantages and disadvantages of doing this. A strong analysis and report from a well-renowned expert can be a powerful persuader.

Deal with your opponent's case and how you will counter your opponent's arguments. Anticipate and be prepared to address these issues as they arise at mediation. Do your research and have it available.

Do your homework on the opponent's expert or potential expert. Verify the expert's degree and licensing. Review any articles or books the expert has written on the subjects involved in your case. Get a history and review transcripts of prior testimony. Trial lawyer associations are a good place to start looking for this information. You might be able to demonstrate that this will be a less than effective witness and that you are prepared to refute the expert's findings.

PRETRIAL ORDER

Keep this order handy for easy and frequent reference. Know your deadlines. The court has given this order for a reason. The court wants to be assured that there will be no last-minute surprises or requests for continuances. Some courts follow this order to the letter. For example, if you have not filed a witness and exhibit list by the date ordered, you may have to rely upon your opponent's list or worse yet, do without. You would be wise to learn the preferences of the court in which you will be appearing. Will they accept filing by fax? Do they need to have the original before they will sign? The court staff may be able to help you with such questions and problems.

DISCOVERY

Review all depositions, Interrogatories, document production, and Requests for Admissions, both your own and your opponent's. Do you need to supplement your responses? Does your opponent need to supplement responses? Have either of you deferred responses until "investigation and discovery are complete"? If so, you must update and/or supplement your responses. This is the time to submit additional discovery to your opponent. You will not have another chance. You must permit 30 days from the discovery cutoff date to allow your opponent time to answer. You might consider using Requests for Admissions at this time to further narrow the issues, to verify the truth of key material facts, and to identify key documents. This is a very valuable and powerful tool if used correctly. Remember, if your opponent—or worse yet, if you—fail to respond within the time allowed, the requests are deemed admitted. If you have carefully and thoughtfully crafted your requests, your opponent could admit liability or admit the authenticity of key documents or pieces of evidence.

Review all the depositions that have been taken to date. You should have summarized and indexed them and know where to find key pieces of information, whether to further your case or to impeach the witness. Schedule and prepare for additional depositions. If necessary, use a master list to keep track of times, places, and completion of depositions. This gives everyone an outline of what is done and what remains to be done, and becomes especially important if several attorneys are involved. Prepare a separate folder for each person to be deposed containing the notice of deposition, court reporter information, outline of questions or areas of questions, and documents that you want to have the witness identify. When all depositions have been completed, prepare a checklist to be used at trial. Do you have the originals? Has the deposition been submitted to the court? If you want the jury to see deposition exhibits, have you prepared copies? What is the court's preference for ruling on deposition objections? Do you need to make arrangements to have a hearing before the trial begins, or would the judge rather rule during the trial?

Prepare or update logs or indexes of pleadings, discovery, documents produced, and medical records and bills, if appropriate.

Compare and contrast all depositions and statements of all parties and witnesses. Look for disparities and similarities. Evaluate the witnesses. Who would be the best for your side? Who is the best at refuting the position of your opponent? Begin to narrow and refine the list of witnesses who will actually testify at trial.

FILE CONTROL

Several weeks before the trial, move the file to your office or to a "war room." Review the file and organize it. You might have to reorganize more than once before the trial actually begins. As you organize, create an index of files and subfiles. When you pack the boxes to transport the file to court, number and label each box noting the contents. Add the numbers to your index, and keep copies in your trial notebook. This will help you to keep track of the total number of boxes and enable you to locate or to direct someone to locate things quickly.

You should identify exhibits you will need and have them copied. Locate memos or transcripts from witness interviews, and place them in the appropriate witness files.

If your case involves an injury, with treatment by health care providers, you may need to gather the most recent medical records or bills. Have them properly authenticated. Where did you get them? Have they been identified in a deposition? Will the doctor be testifying live? If not, you need to lay a foundation for their admissibility. Do you have other documents that need to be properly authenticated; for example, an autopsy report, a coroner's verdict, or a death certificate? Having these documents properly authenticated may prevent having to bring someone to trial to admit them into evidence. It will also save you an enormous amount of time running around the city, state, or country at the last minute to accomplish this. Review the applicable Rules of Evidence.

PLANNING THE "SHOW"

Prepare the trial schedule. Review your witness and exhibit list. If time has not elapsed, do you need to add to it? Some courts want a "realistic" witness and exhibit list before the trial begins. At the very least, they want an estimate of the time it will take each side to present its case. Which witnesses will testify live and which will be by deposition? In what order will the witnesses appear? Tell a story. Keep it logical for the jury. Keep it interesting. Vary between live witnesses and deposition testimony. Consider videotaping some of the depositions. Some witnesses are very impressive when seen and heard, others are better on paper. If you will be using video, make arrangements for playback of the video during trial. If depositions are being read, vary the readers and match the gender of the witness and the reader. Keep it interesting and moving along. It is important to hold the attention of the jury. Trials can be tedious and boring, and anything you can do to keep the attention and interest of the jurors will be appreciated. Build some flexibility into the schedule. Expect the unexpected. It is sometimes difficult to anticipate or estimate the length of testimony when you are planning the order of witnesses. You know how long it will take to read or show a video of a deposition. If a witness concludes testimony faster than anticipated, and the next witness has not yet arrived, you will be able to use the deposition testimony to keep the trial moving along. The court may have some flexibility in scheduling breaks at logical stopping points in the proceeding. If the end of the day is near, and your next witness will be a long one, the court may be happy to end the day early rather than to stay late or interrupt witness testimony.

Contact all witnesses and help them prepare to testify. Provide them with a copy of their deposition. Interview them again. Give them a chance to practice their testimony. Review with them any exhibits that they will introduce. Let them know what to expect in the courtroom. This will be a new experience for lay witnesses and not always a pleasant one. Advise them of the schedule. Try to work around their schedules to the best of your ability. Prepare any necessary subpoenas and witness fees. Some witnesses feel more comfortable if they have been ordered to appear to testify. Some may need the subpoena for their employer. You will be protected if the witness fails to appear. The court can then order them to appear. Avoid long waits for your witnesses. They will be most appreciative and will do a much better job if they have not had to endure a long and boring wait. Be honest with them. As hard as you try, some delay may be unavoidable. Get all phone numbers where the witness may be reached at all times of the day and night. Give them a contact person and number in case they have to reach you while you are at trial. Advise them of changes in the schedule. Be sure to give them directions to the courthouse, and establish a time and place to meet you or to wait for you. Try to meet them in a timely manner to put them at ease and to let them know how much you appreciate their efforts. If you were the one to prepare the witness, allow time for the witness to meet the attorney and to establish a rapport, so they both will feel more comfortable during the examination.

Prepare expert witnesses in much the same way. Review their report with them. Provide them with a checklist or an outline. Do they have all the necessary background information? Review all exhibits that will be introduced through their testimony. Review any charts or blowups that have been created for use during their testimony. You want them to feel comfortable and familiar with items they will be asked to identify. Will they be preparing or providing any of the exhibits? If so, you need to have copies. Do they need to use any special equipment during their testimony? If so, will they provide it, or do you need to make arrangements to have it available? These are questions you should have answered well in advance to allow yourself time to make any special arrangements.

Prepare your clients. This is an extremely important event in their lives, and it can be very stressful. It is very important that they understand the trial process. They probably have never been in a courtroom before. Familiarize them with the setting and the logistics. Explain the role of each person they can expect to see in the courtroom. Instruct them in proper dress and demeanor. Rehearse their testimony. Help them to prepare a chronology and examples of how whatever event has brought them to trial has affected them. This will be helpful not only to them, but to the attorney for use in direct examination of the client. Do a mock cross-examination. Have them review prior deposition statements and their answers to Interrogatories. Review all exhibits that they will introduce. By this time, clients may well know and be more comfortable with you than the attorney. You may be the one they look to for support. Let them know what to expect. You may need to explain parts of the procedure as they develop. For example, let them know that they can expect to hear a motion for a directed verdict at the close of the case. That is something you might take for granted that you may hear, and it is a normal part of the routine for a paralegal, but it comes as a huge and very unexpected and unpleasant surprise to clients to hear someone say that they have not proved their case and it should be dismissed.

EXHIBITS AND DEMONSTRATIVE EVIDENCE

Use demonstrative evidence to illustrate, demonstrate, or re-create an object or event for the jury. Exhibits should add interest, variety, and persuasiveness to witness examinations. They can make witness testimony easier to understand, and they can help to focus the attention of the jurors on specific issues.

Determine the purpose of the visual aid. Keep your theme in mind. Use demonstrative evidence to build your case. If the case involves highly technical information, the judge and jury must be educated. Summarize large amounts of information to make it easier for the witness to explain and the jury to understand.

Visual aids reinforce the spoken testimony. The type of visual aid or demonstrative evidence depends on the type of information the attorney wishes to convey. They can range from the very inexpensive and low-tech to the very expensive and high-tech. Whatever you choose to use, the project should be planned and created accurately and carefully, with great attention to detail. Of course, the type of visual aids you use will depend on the nature of the case and the allotted budget.

Arrange for a pretrial evidentiary hearing if you anticipate a dispute. This can prove to be invaluable. You will know ahead of time if your evidence is admissible, if you will have to approach it from a different angle, or if you will have to start from scratch.

Use summaries, but be sure to have the client or witness review them. You do not want them seeing the summary for the first time on the witness stand.

Make certain you have a proper foundation for each piece of evidence you want to introduce. Do you have the proper witness to introduce the evidence? If you are using demonstrative evidence, have available the appropriate research to support your argument on admissibility.

Stipulate with opposing counsel to as much evidence as possible before the start of the trial, but be prepared in the event that this agreement cannot be reached.

Pre-mark the exhibits if that is the preference of the court, and make a master list with the numbers and description of each exhibit. Leave room for exhibits that may be identified during the course of the trial. Provide the list, identified as yours, to the court reporter. Court reporters really appreciate this and frequently use it as their checklist during the trial, making it easy to compare your list to theirs. If it is neatly prepared on the computer, you will avoid the problem of sometimes illegible handwriting when writing in haste during the course of the trial. Identify and mark blowups of exhibits (some courts want the original introduced before the enlargement).

Make enough copies for the judge, court reporter, witness, each attorney, and each juror. Most courts require this and it is a huge time-saver. Of course, it is impossible for some exhibits to be duplicated and those will have to be passed to or viewed by the jury. It is a good idea, and sometimes required, to provide notebooks of exhibits for the judge, opposing counsel, and each juror. If there is some doubt about an exhibit being introduced or whether it will be admissible, simply make enough three-hole punched copies, and the jury can insert their copies into their notebooks at the proper time. Some courts prefer to handle all exhibits in this manner. This helps the jurors to stay organized, keeps the exhibits handy in one place, and avoids a lot of shuffling of papers and wasted time. Some courts allow the jurors to take the exhibits with them to the jury room, and this is a very efficient method for doing that.

Make arrangements for any exhibits that need special handling. Do you or any of your experts have a very large or heavy exhibit that needs to be delivered? If so, who is handling the arrangements? Do not leave anything to chance.

COURTROOM LOGISTICS

Does the court have a preference where the parties are seated? If not, where would your team be most comfortable? Is there enough room for all of your files and exhibits? Will you need to make arrangements to keep them elsewhere? How will you get everything to the courtroom? Are there elevators? Are carts available? Will you need help? Is there a special entrance you can use to make unloading everything easier? Will the boxes and equipment be searched or scanned? If so, how and where will this be done? What can you do to expedite this procedure?

Will you be allowed to use a copier? Will you have access to a telephone? Check to see if cell phones are allowed in the building. In some jurisdictions, they are not allowed. If you will be using a cell phone, remember to turn it off while in the courtroom. Will you be allowed to use a computer in the courtroom? Some courts do not permit this.

Is there a law library available for your use? If so, what kinds of books and reference materials are available?

Where will you be most comfortable? Will you be sitting at counsel table, or do you need to be free to move around to manage witnesses and details? Is there a place that you can do so easily, quietly, and conveniently without disrupting the proceedings? It can be very distracting to have people moving about and going in and out. Judges and jurors need to be free from distraction to allow them to fully concentrate on the matter at hand.

Ensure that the judge and jury will be able to see and hear everything. Your entire presentation is to them. It is much easier for counsel to move and adjust their position if necessary.

Check with court staff for their preference for pre-marking exhibits. Ask if you will be assigned letters or numbers.

What, if any, equipment do they have available for use during trial? Most courts have a television and VCR or DVD player available for use, but you sometimes have to make arrangements in advance. You may need to provide your own equipment or have a vendor provide and set up the equipment. Work with the court's staff to make the necessary arrangements so there will be no disruption in the proceedings and your case will proceed smoothly.

Check the power sources. Where will you be able to plug in electronic equipment or a computer? Extension cords and three-prong adapters should be included in your trial supplies, but will you need extra ones?

TRIAL NOTEBOOK

Find and develop a system that works for you and your attorney(s). This may mean different systems for different attorneys. It may be in the form of a three-ring notebook or in individual file folders. In organizing witness and exhibit information for trial, one method is to create a separate folder for each witness containing the subpoena, prior deposition, outline of testimony, summaries, résumé or curriculum vitae, and any exhibits that the witness will introduce. (Cross-reference with your exhibit notebook and its index.) Make a notebook for each attorney who will be present at trial.

Tab, label, and index everything. If you will not be sitting at counsel table, it is important that the attorney be able to locate what he or she needs. You might include the following:

- *Pleadings.* This section includes the Complaint and Answer, Cross- or Counterclaims and answers, and any of the above that have been amended.
- *Motions.* This section includes important motions and orders, such as Motions for Summary Judgment or Motions to Quash or to Strike certain evidence. Include also any pertinent legal research.
- *Discovery.* If this is voluminous, you might want to use a separate notebook(s). You should have an extra copy of the responses to use to admit into evidence if necessary.
- *Motions in Limine/pretrial motions.* If there has been an important ruling on a Motion in Limine or other pretrial motion, it can be very important to have that available for handy reference. Discussions and disputes can arise during the course of the trial. Include any applicable legal research.
- *Trial brief.* Even if not required by the court, a trial brief is an excellent way to summarize your case and legal theories, not only for the court but for those presenting the case. Sometimes issues you have been struggling with become clear, and/or solutions are found as you are preparing for trial.
- *Issue instruction.* It is also helpful to prepare an issue instruction. Again, this is not always required by the court, but it is good if the jury can hear your thoughts about the case and its issues. This is the "bare-bones" outline of the case that will be presented to the jury during the preliminary instructions.
- *Preliminary instructions.* Keep copies of the instructions tendered by each side and the court, noting which were offered, which were refused, and which were actually given. Some courts merely use their own instructions for this phase. Include any applicable legal research that may be needed in arguing these instructions.

- *Voir dire.* This is the jury selection phase of the trial. If you were able to get the juror questionnaires in advance of the trial, they should be in this section with any notes or comments made about the panel members. Include an outline of questions or areas of questioning that will be used during the jury selection process. Also include a chart or form that the attorneys can use for this phase.

- O*pening.* This section can include anything from early notes made on the case, to random thoughts the trial team has had, to the actual outline the attorney intends to use during opening statements. This will be the first time the jury has really heard from you about your case. It is very important to give them a clear and concise summary of the case. You might include a chronology of events to use during this summary. Typically, the jury is told how the evidence will unfold. It might be helpful to include a list of witnesses that will be used, along with the key points of their testimony.

- *Witness outlines.* This section should include an outline for each witness, along with pertinent notes. You may build upon this section during the trial if issues come up with a witness that you want to clarify or further explore with later witnesses.

- *Motions on the evidence.* If it is anticipated that a written motion on the evidence or a directed verdict will be made at the end of the case in chief, you should have the motion or a response ready to file, with enough copies for opposing counsel. Include any applicable legal research that may be needed to argue or defend this motion.

- *Opposition witnesses and exhibits.* This section includes outlines and notes for cross-examination. Include pertinent legal research on issues or evidence.

- *Closing and notes for closing.* This section will develop through the trial. While you may include basic information and an outline here before the start of the trial, many things will happen during the trial, and many notes will be made on information to be included in closing arguments.

- *Rebuttal notes.* This section should contain basic information and an outline before trial, but decisions will be made during trial whether to have rebuttal evidence and, if so, what it might be.
- *Final instructions and notes.* As before, keep a complete copy of the instructions offered by each side and the court, noting which were offered, which were refused, and which were actually given. You should include the necessary legal research that may be needed when the instructions are argued. This part of the trial, out of the hearing of the jury, should be made a part of the court's record. Instructions can be an important part of an appeal, and you should have a complete record—the court's and your own notes—of what transpired.
- *Verdict forms.* Some courts do not require or even allow this, but if they do, you should be prepared. Sometimes, subtle changes can have an affect on the jury's ultimate verdict.

You might need to expand the notebook to suit the needs of more complex or specialized cases. You might need to add sections such as a discovery index, outline of liability, outline of damages, analysis of the issues, outline of proof, law and evidence briefs, medical or technical notes, and each summary and/or index that was created to manage the documents or issues of the case.

PARALEGAL TRIAL NOTEBOOK

Create a notebook for yourself. This is probably the most important notebook you will create. It does not have to be a duplicate of the attorney's notebook (though you might want a copy of the attorney's notebook index). Tailor it to suit your needs and your case. You might include the trial schedule, so you will be able to make necessary adjustments, and all witness information, including addresses and telephone numbers, with a copy of witness testimony outlines. You might be the one doing the last-minute preparation with the witnesses. Use a chart or form to track the order of witness testimony. Include your list of exhibits and checklists to track the admission or refusal of each exhibit.

Keep any particularly sensitive or important bits of information in your notebook. You should also have sections for lists of witnesses and exhibits and for collecting notes for use during cross-examinations, rebuttals, or closing.

Create a master list of important telephone and fax numbers and email addresses. It is very important that one or more persons at your office have the pertinent trial information, witness names and contact information, and a general outline of the trial. When problems arise, the office may be the only way a witness has to reach you, and someone needs to be prepared to address these emergencies or to contact you. Have the home telephone numbers of your secretary and each attorney's secretary. You will all be away from the office during normal business hours, and it might be necessary to reach someone after hours. Have the names and numbers of vendors and suppliers for any last-minute emergencies. You might have to create a last-minute exhibit or need a large number of copies made. You should also include the court's telephone and fax numbers to give to anyone who might need to reach you. Include the numbers for opposing counsel. It is sometimes necessary to talk to opposing counsel outside of the regular court hours. Each trial team member should take his or her notebook when they leave the courtroom for the day, so they will have it as they prepare for the next day.

GETTING READY TO MOVE

Prepare to take the case from the office to the court. In the last few days before trial, meet frequently with the trial team. Each person should have his or her own assignments and should be aware of what others on the team are doing. It is important to compare notes. Now is not the time to close the lines of communication. There are usually any number of last-minute details.

You have already organized and indexed the case files, probably more than once. Do an inventory to make sure nothing is missing and everything is still intact. It is now more important than ever to maintain the integrity of the files.

Is everything that is stored in electronic format loaded and ready? Create backups and fail-safe plans. If possible, take more than one laptop in case of technical problems. Check all equipment to ensure that everything is in working order. Take all necessary cords and chargers, along with extra batteries and bulbs.

Have hard copies of presentations and exhibits prepared and ready for use if technical difficulties arise. Do the same with all exhibits. Has everything been copied? Have all exhibits been prepared in final format? Has everything been enlarged that needs to be? Use your exhibit checklist to ensure that you have everything and know where to find it. Leave explicit instructions for exhibits that need to be created after the trial has begun.

You will need many more things in addition to the case files. You might have research and trial rules available on the laptop, but would the attorney prefer his own book that may be tabbed for his or her own easy use? Is there some other research or reference book that might be needed? Compare notes with the trial team to avoid duplication.

You might want to load all the case computer files on the laptop onto a disk or CD-ROM. It is very helpful to have the instructions on a disc to give to the court reporter, who can make necessary changes. Take extra disks or CDs. Make sure you have an extension cord and three-prong adapter in case your battery goes out.

Pack extra office supplies. You will need extra legal pads and pens. You might need tape, markers, clips, or any number of other things that you normally have handy at your desk. Even if your office is nearby, it can be too far if you need something immediately. Take everything with you. If you do not, you can be sure that the one thing you absolutely have to have will be back at your office.

SHOW TIME

Now is the time to put into action the plan you made when you checked out the courtroom. Have everything delivered to the courthouse, and be available to unpack and organize as needed. Unpack and organize the witness files and the exhibits. Check all the electronic equipment to see that it is functioning properly. If the trial begins as soon as the jury is seated, you must have prepared in advance.

During voir dire, observe the panel members and listen to their answers as they are questioned. Your trial team already has some idea of what kind of jurors they would like to have. They may have a preference about age, gender, or occupation. Your observations can be very important. You will have a different perspective than the attorney and the client. We all react differently to people and situations. You may have a very strong positive or negative reaction to someone that could be an important factor in selecting or rejecting a juror.

In the courtroom, you should observe the decorum, rules, and customs of the court. If the judge requires or prefers that men wear suits and that women wear dresses in the courtroom, now is not the time for you to make a statement for women's rights. If the court does not allow paralegals to be seated at counsel table or the use of a computer in the courtroom, you must honor those rules. While some rules may seem petty, unfair, or even foolish, you should do nothing that might detract from the presentation of your client's case. As you settle into the routine of trial, everyone will become more comfortable in that setting. You will have planned and prepared to make your portion of the trial go as smoothly as possible. You should move about the courtroom as little as possible, making every effort to be quiet and unobtrusive. You should not eat or drink in the courtroom. You should do nothing to distract the jurors. As you are observing them, they will be observing you, your client, and the other members of your trial team. Be courteous and polite at all times to the court and staff, to the opposing counsel and trial team, and to your own client and trial team. Understand and appreciate the dignity and solemnity of the situation that brought all of you to this time and place and proceeding that will ultimately resolve the problem.

Plan to use scheduled breaks to communicate with the attorneys and client. Also use these times to communicate with your office. Check with the attorneys' secretaries. Do they need to speak to the attorney or can you convey messages? Are there matters to be handled back at the office? Determine how and when this will be accomplished and who will be responsible for doing so. Some attorneys will want to hear every detail, and others will be comfortable relying on you to make the right calls. Take advantage of those times to do such things as plan for upcoming witnesses or have the proper exhibits ready. At the beginning and/or end of each day, clean up and organize your area. Assess and regroup with the attorney. Do you need to make adjustments in the next day's schedule? Prepare for the next day's witnesses. Take with you everything you and the trial team will need for overnight review and planning. Review with the court reporter the exhibits that were admitted or refused. Were they passed to the jury? It is sometimes necessary to point out that an exhibit about to be passed to the jury was not admitted or that an exhibit has not been examined by the jury.

GRAND FINALE

The attorney making the closing argument will want time to prepare closing remarks. Use this time to clean up, organize, and pack away everything that will not be needed during the closing. Prepare and organize all exhibits that will be used. Make last-minute blowups of crucial instructions, portions of testimony, and the like. If there are timing concerns, understand the time allotted. If you are the party with the burden of proof, will you be splitting your closing? If you need to time part of the closing, do you have a watch or clock that is readily observable from your vantage point? Plan the signals that will be used, and be sure that each person understands the time he or she will be allowed, the warning if one will be used, and the signal.

At the close of the proceeding, pack and remove everything you can from the courtroom. You will not be needing it again and should not wait for the jury to return its verdict to do this. If you will be leaving the courthouse, provide the court with numbers where you can be reached. When the jury returns its verdict, you should maintain your composure and observe the dignity of the proceeding. Whether or not they have found in your client's favor, the jury had a formidable task in listening to all of the evidence as it was presented, evaluating that evidence, and arriving at a decision. They should be afforded the respect they deserve. If the court allows and the jury is willing, your trial team may or may not choose to talk to jurors after the verdict.

Immediately following the trial, be sure your clients understand what has just occurred in the courtroom. Rejoice with them if you won, and sympathize with them if you lost. Make sure they get answers to their questions, either from you or the attorney.

Thank any witnesses and support personnel at the courthouse and at your office for their contributions to the trial. Complete charts, forms, or indexes pertaining to the last day of trial while the events are fresh in your mind. It is important to have an accurate and complete record in case there is an appeal. Make notes about the jury's findings and any last-minute observations or recollections.

Celebrate or commiserate with the trial team. Win or lose, you have all worked very hard to make the best possible presentation.

In the following week, send letters of appreciation to experts, witnesses, and others who helped in the trial preparation. Don't forget those on your office staff who pitched in to help.

Calendar a date to close the file after all post-trial deadlines have passed.

TAKING THE SHOW ON THE ROAD

An out-of-town trial can be incredibly stressful and hectic. It is important that team members know each other and work well together. It is not a time for the inexperienced. You will be working and living in close quarters during the next days and weeks, and you will be doing so in less than ideal conditions. All the planning and organization previously discussed becomes even more essential when the trial is out of town. You will need to do even more to ensure the smooth transition of the case from the office to the court. The paralegal's role is greatly expanded before and during an out-of-town trial. You will need to take care of many more details, still keeping an eye on the big picture. You will be responsible for more people and more things, with less room for error.

It is doubly important to check with the court and staff before arriving for trial. You should try to meet them before the trial begins. They may have rules, customs, or practices of which you are unaware. Determine the start and end times for the trial day. Does the judge have regularly scheduled lunch and other breaks? Should the attorneys arrive early to work on procedural matters? Where should witnesses report? Is there a place in the courthouse where you can meet and talk to witnesses? Can they recommend support services you can use while in their town? Can they recommend places to stay or where to eat? Once the trial starts, you will probably not have time to wander around looking for a quick sandwich or a 24-hour copy center.

If you will be driving back and forth each day, familiarize yourself with the best travel routes. Where are the gas stations? Where should you park each day? Some towns are very confusing with many twists and turns or one-way streets. And you do not want to leave court at the end of the day to find that your car has been towed because you parked improperly.

If you will be staying for the duration of the trial, select a hotel and check out their facilities. Is there a desk or work table in the rooms? Is there adequate lighting in the rooms? You don't want a 60-watt bulb if you are working, reading, and getting ready for trial. You may have to bring extra lamps or bulbs. Do they have office equipment or a business center you can use? You will need access to a fax and copy machines. Will you need to bring or lease equipment? You will want to bring your own computer and printer. Will there be adequate phone and Internet lines? Is there enough space for all of your boxes and piles of files, materials, and exhibits that you cannot leave in the courtroom? Will you need an extra room, or is there another place to store things?

Make travel arrangements and reservations. Will you need to rent a van or arrange to ship everything you must bring with you to maintain your office on the road? You will need to determine the best providers of these services and make the necessary arrangements.

Will you need to arrange for office space and secretarial assistance? Is there a law library you will be able to use? The local or state bar association may have a roster of available services.

Get a copy of the local telephone directory with yellow pages. Look at the first several pages for maps, emergency medical help, and other useful information. The Internet is an invaluable resource in locating maps and directions, checking the weather conditions, and locating services and suppliers, restaurants, drugstores, dry cleaners, banks, office supplies, and copy centers. You can accomplish a great deal of legal research online. Be familiar with what is available and how to find it.

If you have local counsel, do they have facilities available for your use? Can you utilize their staff if needed? Get to know the staff and the layout of their office. Establish a contact person. If you will need to access their office after hours, determine how best to do that.

When you begin to pack for the trial, include extra office supplies or equipment. Look at your desk and in the supply area. Take everything you think you might need or want. Do not forget to take other supplies you would take for granted at home including tissues, Band-Aids, and headache, stomach, cough, and cold remedies. Remind everyone to pack extra glasses or contacts and prescription medication. Include extra surge protectors, batteries, and charging equipment for cell phones and laptops. Take manuals for computers and software programs.

Expand your telephone contact list to include home numbers of trial team members. Include the numbers of several associates you can call if you need research support in the evening. You might need phone and beeper numbers for computer- and other equipment-support people. You should leave your contact information with your office. Be sure your secretaries and the receptionist know what is going on and how to locate you. Include phone, fax, and email numbers for the hotel, court, or anywhere else you might be reached. It is more important than ever to check in with your office, preferably twice a day. You need to know that everything is being handled, and they will want to hear how all of you are doing and how the trial is progressing. You are the contact person and must be available. You must also provide your contact information to your witnesses, along with maps, directions, and travel information. Be sure to provide them with a map of the courthouse, including parking information.

You might want to prepare a special box or file with critical exhibits or information that you will keep with you at all times. Do not trust that a shipping or delivery service will get everything to you when you need it. If you have an original copy of the "smoking gun," do not entrust it to anyone else. At no time is a paralegal's responsibility for documents more crucial than when the trial is on the road.

Make a packing list for each member of the trial team and support staff. They can review it and remind you of things you might have forgotten. Use the final list at the end of the trial to ensure that everything gets back to the office.

Keep careful and accurate records of expenditures, experts' time, and anything else you will have to review with the client at the close of the trial. Plan to settle up with your contractors (secretarial support, copy center bills, etc.) before leaving town. How will you do this? Do you have a firm credit card, and can you sign? Will someone need to write a check? You will need to plan for these and other possible needs that may arise before you leave your office.

While a trial on the road is a lot of work, it is not without its rewards. You will have the opportunity to increase your skills and expertise. You will learn to anticipate what is needed by each member of the trial team at each step of the proceeding. You will earn the respect and confidence of the other members of the trial team. They will recognize the vital role you played in preparing for and bringing the trial to completion. If it had not been experienced before, this trial will have demonstrated the importance, the necessity, and the merits of working as a team. After successful completion of a long and exhausting trial on the road, every other trial will seem relatively routine.

POST-TRIAL

Trial work is both exhilarating and exhausting. In the final phase of trial preparation, your team concentrates their energies and focuses on matters related to the trial. During the trial, your full attention is focused on the courtroom events as they unfold. You will spend your days managing the daily details, logistics, and problems of presenting the trial. There will be at least a few days when you are required to operate at a hectic pace. Depending on the size of the case, there may be many more days of this routine. All these days of intense concentration can take a lot out of you. Win or lose, you may feel a physical and mental letdown. It may be difficult to get back into your regular schedule and routine after the excitement of trial. You will need to find a way to reenergize and refocus, especially if the trial has been lengthy or grueling. This might mean taking a few hours or days to rest and relax away from the office or to pursue whatever activities you enjoy. Get back in touch with your family and friends, and find out what is going on in the rest of the world. When you return, you will be able to think more clearly, and you will be refreshed and ready to tackle whatever has been piling up on your desk in your absence!

Chapter 6
Areas of Practice

PARALEGALS ARE VITAL MEMBERS of the legal team in all areas of practice. This chapter discusses some (but not all) areas of law in which paralegals are utilized and provides an overview of some of the various tasks that paralegals may perform in each area once the attorney has established the attorney/client relationship and set the fee to be charged. This chapter will provide some insight into what paralegals in these types of settings do and will offer suggestions, where appropriate, for ways to improve one's skills or knowledge in that particular area.

The National Federation of Paralegal Associations, Inc. (NFPA) has available on its website, at *www.paralegals.org*, a handbook titled "Paralegal Responsibilities" (© 1996). This handbook provides a detailed listing by practice area of specific tasks that paralegals may perform. The National Association of Legal Assistants (NALA), in its Model Standards and Guidelines for Utilization of Legal Assistants/Paralegals, Guideline 5, at *www.nala.org/News.htm*, lists general functions that a paralegal may perform under the supervision of an attorney and as delegated by the attorney. The American Bar Association Standing Committee on Paralegals (ABA SCOP), in Guidelines 2 and 3 of the ABA Model Guidelines for the Utilization of Paralegal Services, at *www.abanet.org/legalservices/ paralegals*, describes those tasks that attorneys may and may not delegate to a paralegal. Specifically, an attorney may not delegate responsibility for establishing the attorney/client relationship, setting the amount of fee to be charged, rendering a legal opinion, or any other task proscribed to a nonlawyer by statute, court rule, administrative rule or regulation, controlling authority, the applicable rule of professional conduct of the jurisdiction in which the lawyer practices, or as set forth in the guidelines themselves. These examples show that paralegals can be utilized in all areas of the law and further, that paralegals are essential to the delivery of cost-efficient and quality legal services.

DOMESTIC RELATIONS/FAMILY LAW

Domestic relations/family law may be one of the largest areas of paralegal utilization in the United States. It includes, but is not limited to, divorce, legal separation, custody and visitation, paternity, and adoption. For the purposes of this section, when we refer to family law paralegals, we will concentrate mainly on the issue of divorce or dissolution of marriage. Family law paralegals normally become involved in these cases at the very beginning and are essential in helping to provide cost-effective legal services to clients. Family law paralegals usually perform the following types of tasks:

- Interview clients for information necessary to draft a petition, counterpetition, or response thereto
- Collect detailed financial information from the client including income, benefits, assets and liabilities, gifts and inheritances, and so forth
- Assist the client in preparing an accurate listing of, and analyzing, monthly income and expenses

- Determine spousal support requirements, calculate child support, and draft income-withholding orders
- Draft discovery requests and responses, including discovery requests to nonparties, to obtain information regarding assets, liabilities, income, and deferred compensation plans (e.g., retirement plans, IRAs, etc.)
- Draft petitions, affidavits, and proposed orders for restraining and protective orders, and responses thereto
- Draft motions and proposed orders for hearings and relief
- Assist, as necessary, with researching and obtaining expert witnesses, private investigators, parenting time coordinators, counselors, and the like and getting reports
- Docket, and notify clients of, hearings and deadlines associated with the case
- Work with the attorney and client to prepare the client and case for hearing, mediation, and/or trial (includes such things as drafting pre-mediation statements, proposed stipulations, exhibits, and trial presentations)
- Draft settlement documents, qualified domestic relations orders, quitclaim deeds, and other documents related to the transfer of tangible and intangible property after the dissolution is final
- Draft petitions to modify previous orders of the court and draft proposed orders for the same

Family law paralegals are often in daily contact with the client. Paralegals relay questions and information between the attorney and client, answer procedural questions, relay information to and from the court, and draft and prepare documents in final form for review and signature by the attorney (first) and client (once approved by the attorney). Paralegals may also prepare the signed documents for filing with the clerk and service on opposing counsel; correspond with opposing counsel and the court, mediator, expert witnesses, and nonparties as appropriate; interview witnesses; perform research; and assist the attorney at mediation and/or the final hearing.

A good family law paralegal will know how to calculate child support, will create exhibits for mediation and hearing, and will be able to provide the attorney with documented details about the case, as needed.

In a dissolution of marriage, information regarding the income of each party, including assets, gifts and inheritances, business interests, and monthly expenses, is extremely important. Many times, clients are reluctant to provide the degree of detail that is required, and it is important to explain to them that the attorney must have this information in order to accurately represent the client's best interest. In many jurisdictions, if something is discovered after the divorce is final, the case can be reopened in order to address the asset or debt that was left out. This could potentially result in a party being sanctioned by the court if the court finds there is sufficient cause to do so.

Some jurisdictions require each party to prepare and file a document that provides information regarding the party's individual income and that lists all assets and debts of which the party is aware—both individual and joint. This document may be called a financial declaration (or various other titles), and the client may be required to sign it under oath. This document provides the court with important financial information early in the case, among other things, to assist the court in the determination of temporary child support and spousal maintenance. This document will then form the basis for drafting a marital estate exhibit, which is a spreadsheet that is utilized in settlement negotiations, at mediation, and/or at the final hearing. The marital estate exhibit should list every asset and debt that existed at a particular point in time (often the date of filing), including gifts and inheritances if those items are included in the jurisdiction in which you work, the value of each asset, and the amount of each debt, and then give a net value of the overall marital estate. The marital estate exhibit can be used to create a proposed division of the assets and debts by adding columns for the husband and wife and delineating which items go in each column. Utilizing formulas, the spreadsheet can automatically calculate the percentage of net marital estate allocated to each party, for example, 45 percent to the husband and 55 percent to the wife.

A sample financial declaration and marital estate exhibit can be found in appendix B.

Many jurisdictions have software programs that have been specifically designed around their particular child support guidelines and requirements, and many states offer online child support calculators that can be utilized by a paralegal or attorney to calculate child support payments. However, there is more to calculating child support than just entering numbers into a program. The paralegal has an obligation to review and understand that jurisdiction's requirements regarding child support. In order to properly utilize such programs, the paralegal must, among other things, have at least a basic understanding of what is and is not allowable income for each parent, the applicable deductions (e.g., children from a former or subsequent relationship), items that qualify as extraordinary educational and/or health care expenses, day care expenses, and when or how much income may be imputed to an unemployed or underemployed parent.

Family law paralegals should review case law and understand the opinions set forth therein. It is a good idea to create a computer or hard-copy file of significant decisions as they are handed down by the high court in your jurisdiction for future reference. Whether saved in hard copy or electronic form, the decisions can be sorted according to subject type with a cross-reference to the significant points. Be sure to include the case citation and the date handed down, and provide sufficient information in your coding so that if something is overturned, you will be able to find it and get rid of it. Nothing is worse than relying on bad law.

Kelly Blue Book, NADA Guides, and the Automobile Association Red Book are all good examples of available resources for obtaining values of automobiles, motorcycles, and other motor vehicles. Some of these sources are available online or may be part of a firm's library. To use these sources, you will need to know the make, model, and year of the vehicle and/or have the vehicle identification number (VIN). This number can be found on the vehicle title or registration and is also accessible online from the Bureau of Motor Vehicles. Once you have located information regarding the potential value of the client's automobile(s), be sure to provide the attorney and client with that information so that, together, they can make the final decision regarding its value. In the case of a collector automobile, you may need to locate an expert to provide a written appraisal.

Family law paralegals often have a listing of appraisers for valuing real and personal property. Check with other paralegals in your firm and/or the attorney before contacting someone. It is imperative to find out what the appraiser charges for his or her services and to obtain the attorney's approval before hiring the appraiser. In some instances, the parties will prefer to agree to a value rather than incur the cost of hiring a third party to make an appraisal.

Many jurisdictions these days require the parties in a dissolution where there are children to attend a type of dissolution workshop. The workshop may go by different names, but the general purpose is to make the parents aware of how divorce affects children and to give the parents some suggestions and guidance in dealing with the children and each other. Generally, the workshop is mandatory and must be completed before the final divorce will be granted. Fees for the workshop are minimal, and in hardship circumstances, the fees can be waived.

In addition to the workshop mentioned above, it has become common for the courts to order the parties in a dissolution to mediation. Then, if mediation fails, the court will set a date for a final hearing. In preparing for mediation, the family law paralegal will normally draft a pre-mediation statement for the client setting forth information regarding the parties and any children, the procedural and factual history of the case, the major issues such as custody and visitation or the need for spousal maintenance, the earning capabilities of each party, and a brief description of any settlement negotiations to date. Usually, the mediator will also be provided with a copy of the marital estate exhibit and a proposed division, which may be sent to the mediator along with the pre-mediation statement or provided to the mediator on the day of mediation.

Sometimes the paralegal will attend the mediation along with the client and attorney. The responsibilities of the paralegal at mediation will depend on the practice of the attorney and firm. Many clients are nervous at mediation, and the paralegal may need to provide emotional support. In some instances, the paralegal is there mainly because he or she is more familiar with the file itself and can quickly locate information and documents requested by the attorney and mediator. In addition, the paralegal may be needed to update the marital estate division spreadsheet as the mediation progresses in order to keep track of the agreed upon division of the assets and debts.

PROBATE AND ESTATE

Probate and estates includes wills and trusts, and relate to both the drafting and administration of the same. With a few exceptions, litigation related to these matters would be handled much the same as any other type of litigation. The following list, which is by no means comprehensive, is an example of some of the tasks a probate and estate paralegal would perform:

- Trusts
  - Coordinate transfer of tangible and intangible assets into trusts
  - Draft fiduciary and intangible property tax returns
  - Coordinate periodic income and principle distributions
  - Draft trust documents, *inter vivos* agreements, and testamentary trust provisions for wills
  - Correspond and communicate with trust grantors and beneficiaries
  - Obtain tax identification number for trusts
  - Maintain financial records
  - Draft pleadings registering or terminating trusts and appointing or substituting trustees
  - Draft inventories, accounts, and petitions for trusts requiring adjudication

- Estate administration
  - o Review will and draft necessary documents to file will with probate court and/or to commence a probate proceeding
  - o Obtain or assist executor in obtaining certified copies of death certificate
  - o Assist in locating all heirs, devisees, beneficiaries, and other interested parties
  - o Assist in locating and evaluating assets (as of date of death and alternate valuation date); verify bank balances and prepare inventory
  - o Arrange for notice to creditors for publication in newspaper
  - o Determine when formal appraisals are necessary and arrange the same
  - o Maintain estate records and draft estate, fiduciary income, gift, and inheritance tax returns, as necessary
  - o Review pertinent documents and perform research as needed relating to tax filings
  - o Draft miscellaneous petitions for such things as spousal allowances, permission to purchase grave markers, paying debts and expenses of the estate, etc.
  - o Draft interim reports, final settlement and distribution documents, etc.
  - o Ensure that assets are properly transferred

Paralegals also participate in the drafting of wills and in the administration of conservatorships and guardianships.

In drafting a will, the paralegal may need to contact the client for additional information related to property or heirs and/or to clarify exactly how the property should be distributed. The paralegal may also draft living wills and/or appointments of health care representatives to be executed in conjunction with the will, codicils or addendums to already existing wills, and general durable powers of attorney, for example. In addition, the paralegal often participates in the execution and witnessing of these estate planning documents.

In conservatorships and guardianships, paralegals participate in client conferences, correspond and communicate with the guardian/conservator regarding the proceeding and estate, and draft pleadings to establish, report on, and terminate the same. Interim reports, accountings, and inventories must be prepared and filed, and these are usually paralegal tasks.

For all of the matters involved in probate and estate administration, it is imperative that the paralegal be aware of and docket deadlines associated with each type of matter. For instance, in estate planning, there are specific deadlines for the filing of inheritance tax returns, federal estate tax returns, and so forth. Guardianships will require periodic reports. Depending on the jurisdiction and perhaps the type of guardianship, these reports must be filed every six months, once a year, or every other year.

The paralegal must review the statutes and rules for the jurisdiction in which the paralegal works to be certain that all deadlines and requirements are being met. When doing so, be sure to note the parameters for any situation in which a deadline might not pertain to a particular matter. For instance, many jurisdictions have different rules and deadlines for small estate administration than exist for traditional estate administration. Checklists exist for estates and guardianships to help in meeting deadlines, and of course, there are also software programs available that will do the same. Be sure to check periodically for statutory or local rule changes so you can update your checklists, as needed. Statutory changes most often take effect in January and July of each year.

Some examples of litigation in this area include: will contest; petition to remove/replace trustee, executor, or guardian; and wrongful death. Sometimes an estate or guardianship will become involved in a lawsuit that was pending prior to the establishment of the estate or guardianship and in which the deceased or incompetent was a party.

CORPORATE

There are two types of paralegals that fall under the description of corporate: those who work in law firms that do corporate work and those who work in-house for the corporations themselves. Most large corporations have in-house legal departments where paralegals are assigned to litigation or other activities. This section will deal mainly with the formation and maintenance of corporations and other business entities. These tasks may be performed by either law firm or in-house corporate paralegals, and this section is by no means a comprehensive listing of what can or cannot be performed by the paralegals in either arena.

The following tasks are associated with the formation of corporate entities:

- Check name availability and reserve or register corporate name
- Draft and file articles/certificate of incorporation and bylaws
- Draft documents necessary to issue stock, including but not limited to, subscription agreements, stock certificates, receipts, restrictive legends, and investment letters
- Maintain the corporate minute book
- Draft minutes of organizational meeting of incorporators, stockholders, or board of directors or written consents in lieu of meetings
- Prepare and file documents necessary to obtain local licenses or permits, federal employer identification numbers, assumed business name certificates, applications for professional or special purpose corporations, and/or appropriate Internal Revenue Service applications for formation of nonprofit corporations and tax exempt status
- Draft employment agreements and confidentiality agreements for corporate officers and key employees
- Draft stockholders agreements, lease agreements, or buy-sell agreements

After a corporation is established, there are certain tasks required to maintain the entity and keep it in good standing. To that end, paralegals are involved in drafting amendments to the corporate documents (bylaws, articles of incorporation, stockholders agreements, etc.), filing annual or biennial reports with the secretary of state, and drafting resolutions for consideration by the board members and stockholders. Paralegals are also instrumental in drafting notices, proxy materials, ballots, affidavits of mailing, and agendas for annual and special meetings of stockholders. Paralegals sometimes attend and assist at corporate meetings and draft minutes of meetings.

Corporate paralegals may also be involved in the drafting and filing of documents related to intellectual property of the corporation, as well as Uniform Commercial Code (UCC) financing statements and subsequent amendments, assignments, or terminations with appropriate state and local agencies.

One other very important task that some corporate paralegals perform is to draft the documents, correspondence, and forms necessary to adopt qualified profit sharing, 401(k) and/or pension plans, and related trust agreements and submit these documents to the Internal Revenue Service for determination letters. For this reason, paralegals who work in this specific category of corporate work tend to have specialized training. They also draft summary plan descriptions, employee benefit plans, and necessary notices to plan participants.

Many of the same tasks associated with corporations are necessary to create and maintain partnerships and limited liability companies, but of course, the actual documents will vary. Partnership agreements must be drafted for both limited and general partnerships. Articles of incorporation must be created for limited liability companies. Annual reports and filings will need to be made through the secretary of state, and records of meetings and minutes must be kept just as with corporations. In some instances, noncompetition agreements and amendments will be needed, as will documents necessary to register or qualify the entity in foreign jurisdictions.

Naturally, the larger the business entity, the more work there will be to maintain it, and the more deadlines there will be to keep track of. Remember, the U.S. Securities and Exchange Commission (SEC) *at www.sec.gov*

allows free searches of the EDGAR database, which provides detailed information regarding public companies and their filings, including names and contact information of owners and officers and even downloadable copies of actual filings. Paralegals who work for public corporations will often be responsible for submitting filings to and drafting responses to requests for information from the SEC. Corporate paralegals may also need to track patent or trademark information pertaining to their company. This information can be obtained from the United States Patent and Trademark Office (USPTO) website at *www.uspto.gov/main/profiles/acadres.htm* and will be discussed further in the next section.

As with any other area of law, it is important to docket all upcoming deadlines and annual filings and to set up a system of reminders so that there is sufficient time to prepare and file the necessary documents prior to any such due date. Most law firms and corporations will have a docketing and/or tickler system in place. Work with the attorney to be sure that all deadlines and filings are accounted for. Failure to meet deadlines or file the appropriate documents could harm the corporation, which in turn could result in a malpractice suit and/or disciplinary proceeding against the attorney.

INTELLECTUAL PROPERTY

Copyright, patent, and trademark, more generically referred to as "intellectual property" (IP), is also a very specialized area of law. Consequently, IP paralegals are often highly trained and experienced in the work they do. IP paralegals may perform the following general duties:

- Research and compile information pertaining to national and international intellectual property rights, procedural matters and case law, and unfair copyright and infringement actions
- Coordinate international filings with foreign law offices or other foreign entities; act as liaison with foreign offices
- Maintain docket system of due dates for actions and responses, renewals and oppositions, affidavits, and other related

documents and payments both in the United States and in
foreign countries
- Assist in IP-related litigation
- Assist in oppositions, interferences, and cancellations, including the drafting of any necessary documents related thereto

In addition, IP paralegals perform online searches of USPTO records and
industry databases, and they do general legal research; conduct searches for
information regarding trademarks; draft and file trademark applications and
related and subsequent documents; draft responses to USPTO actions and
oppositions; and watch for potential infringements of clients' trademarks. IP
paralegals also work with their counterparts in foreign countries regarding the
filing and maintenance of foreign trademarks and actions related thereto.

In regard to copyright, paralegals are instrumental in the drafting and
filing of renewal applications, infringement letters, and licensing agreements (and review of proposed licensing agreements); in the review of client
materials and copyright notices (as well as helping to make sure the client
does not infringe on the copyright of another); and in the researching and
compiling of information related to notice requirements, enforcement lon-
gevity, and options for renewal of a copyright.

As with any other area of law, in the event of litigation, an IP paralegal
should have at least some knowledge of the courts and litigation procedures
because the paralegal is likely to be involved in the compilation, review, and
production of electronically stored information.

REAL ESTATE

Real estate is another area where paralegals may wish to specialize. Many
paralegals work in this area, and there is a great deal that paralegals can
do. Deeds, affidavits, and many other real estate documents are drafted
by paralegals for review and approval by attorneys. Upon receipt of title
work, the experienced paralegal will review it, and then proceed to draft

the necessary documents. An experienced real estate paralegal will rarely need to ask the attorney what to do in advance. Rather, he or she will know what to do based on the information contained in the title work. Upon completion, the title work and documents will be forwarded to the attorney for review and approval; if the attorney believes something more needs to be done, then the attorney will notify the paralegal of the same.

It is important to note that real estate law, and the things that paralegals may do in relation thereto, varies greatly from state to state. Consequently, the following information is not meant to be an all-encompassing review of real estate law or procedures in the United States; rather, these are examples of documents that paralegals may draft for review and approval by attorneys depending on the jurisdiction in which the paralegal works. This author's experience is solely based on experience and procedures in the State of Indiana and under the supervision of an attorney.

Warranty deeds transfer title and interest in property, whereas a quit-claim deed simply conveys an interest that may or may not exist. Warranty deeds are used in the purchase and sale of property—they transfer complete title and ownership. Quitclaim deeds are utilized to transfer whatever interest an individual or entity may have in the subject real estate. A person does not have to actually be on the title to quitclaim interest in the property. One common usage of the quitclaim deed is when a husband and wife divorce—many times one party will retain sole ownership of the real estate, and the other party will quitclaim his or her interest in the property in return for payment of a portion of the equity. There may be other situations that call for a quitclaim deed rather than a warranty deed. Please be sure to make note of the particular practice in your jurisdiction and the preferences of your employer.

A survivorship affidavit is sometimes utilized when one of the owners to real estate passes away. It normally includes all of the owners' names and the relationship of the parties, the date that title was taken, a reference to the recording information and instrument, the name and date of death of the deceased, and the legal description and street address of the real estate, and it verifies that that title is retained by the remaining owner(s). It is recorded so that the county or local government and anyone performing a title search will know who the current owner(s) is/are, and for tax and assessment purposes. Many times, however, this document will only be created upon the sale of property; and in some jurisdictions, it is acceptable to insert specific survivorship language into the warranty deed rather than create a separate survivorship affidavit.

A "one-and-the-same" affidavit is prepared when an individual who owns real estate changes his or her name and wishes for the title to be accurately reflected. In the event of refinancing, the lending institution may require the affidavit to be executed and recorded if the owner's name has changed since he or she took title or if the person's name on the mortgage instrument is slightly different from how it is listed on the deed. Like the survivorship affidavit, this affidavit will normally include the name of the individual when he or she took title and the date title was obtained, the legal description and street address of the real estate, a reference to the recording information and instrument, and a statement that sets forth, for example, that "Mary Jane Doe" is one and the same person as "Mary J. Doe," now known as "Mary Jane Doe-Smith."

An offer for purchase of real estate is not the same as a real estate contract. An offer for purchase of real estate is a form normally used and prepared by realtors when someone wants to make an offer to purchase a home or land that is listed for sale. This document is then accepted by the seller, or a counteroffer may be made, or it may be rejected completely. In some instances, there may be several counteroffers back and forth between the seller and potential buyer before a final agreement is reached.

A contract for sale of real estate (real estate contract) is sometimes used when a purchaser, for whatever reason, does not purchase the property outright or obtain a mortgage on the property. Instead, the parties negotiate terms and then execute a contract whereby the purchaser pays a down payment and then makes regular payments toward the balance of the purchase price. A certain amount of interest is usually charged, and the contract is for a specific time period. At the end of that time, the purchaser must either pay the balance in full or obtain a mortgage on the property. Because this is a contract, the terms and provisions are negotiable and dependent on the particular situation of the buyer and seller involved. Again, this is a document that most experienced real estate paralegals can prepare for the attorney's review and approval.

Real estate paralegals may also draft a lease or lease with option to purchase and documents utilized at the closing on the sale of real estate, including, but not limited to, promissory notes, seller's affidavits, mortgages, loan cancellation notices, and settlement statements. In some jurisdictions, nonlawyers may actually perform the closing, and in other jurisdictions, only attorneys may do so. Be sure to check the rules and regulations for the jurisdiction in which you work so that you are compliant with all applicable laws.

As with any other area of law, there are various forms of litigation. From foreclosure to quiet title actions and boundary disputes, paralegals are invaluable members of the legal team.

PERSONAL INJURY

Personal injury is a general description for the area of law that encompasses such things as slip and fall accidents, automobile crashes, train wrecks, and so forth. This general type of personal injury is what this section will discuss; however, it is important to know that there are other types of more specialized personal injury. On-the-job injuries fall under workers compensation claims; toxic torts relate to exposure to toxic chemicals; product liability involves injuries received from a faulty product, machine, or equipment; and medical malpractice, another specialized area that varies greatly from state to state, refers to damages received through the accidental or negligent actions of health care providers.

The personal injury paralegal is usually involved at the very beginning of the case. It is normally the paralegal's responsibility to obtain information regarding such things as the client's (or opposing party's) injuries and medical history, health care providers, and physical restrictions. Once the initial information has been obtained, the paralegal will often review the statutes and/or case law applicable to the situation and draft the Complaint for damages, which may or may not include a request for loss of consortium, lost wages, or other matters. Depending on the circumstances of the injury, the Complaint may be based on a claim of negligence, intentional tort, or the like. If you are unsure of the category of the claim, be sure to discuss it with the attorney and then draft appropriate language for the Complaint.

Generally, a Complaint must state the names of each party, provide enough information to satisfy the jurisdictional requirements of the court, and give a brief description of what occurred, including a statement that one party was injured and the other party is at fault. Jurisdiction is accomplished in several ways, but would normally depend on where the accident occurred, the domicile of each party, and/or the amount of damages involved.

Oftentimes, discovery is initiated early in a personal injury case—sometimes immediately after service of the complaint and summons. Discovery requests to the injured party will request information and documentation related to the plaintiff's injury, medical and work history (including questions designed to determine any preexisting medical conditions), health care providers, hospitals and clinics where treatment was received, permanent impairment, lost wages, relationships (if a loss of consortium is included), any previous accidents or personal injury claims, previous or pending lawsuits in which the plaintiff was/is involved, criminal history, and so forth, and a description of what happened to cause the plaintiff's injury(ies). Unless there is *prima facie* evidence that the defendant is totally at fault, discovery to the plaintiff should also include questions intended to determine the degree of fault of the plaintiff and whether or not the plaintiff attempted to mitigate his or her damages in any way.

Discovery requests to the defendant generally ask for information and documentation related to any claims or defenses the defendant may have raised in his or her Answer to the Complaint, a description of what happened, the amount(s) and type(s) of insurance coverage available, criminal history, any previous accidents or claims made against the defendant, and any other pending or previous lawsuits in which the defendant is a party. If this was a motor vehicle accident, the defendant's driving record should be inquired about. In instances where the mental health of either the plaintiff or defendant is an issue, special interrogatories and requests for production should be drafted to request information about that as well.

Another major responsibility of personal injury paralegals is to gather medical records. To do so, you must first get the basic information regarding the injured party, including the party's name, address, date of birth, and social security number, and a listing of his or her primary care and treating physicians and any hospitals or clinics where the plaintiff was treated. In order to obtain medical records, you must either provide the health care provider with an authorization to release medical records (release form) signed by the plaintiff or serve a nonparty request for production of documents.

The medical release must meet all state and federal requirements for release of medical information. Most hospitals and many of the large health care providers will have their own form that must be used. Generally, you can request the form be faxed or emailed to you so that you can then save it on your computer or file a hard copy for use in future cases. Consider making a folder with copies of the releases required by the various health care providers. In addition, the firm or corporation you work for should have a generic form that can be used for most physicians and another for hospitals or clinics. Again, you will need to make sure the form complies with all requirements of the Health Insurance Portability and Accountability Act, otherwise known as HIPPA. For more information on HIPPA, you can go to the website of the U.S. Department of Health and Human Services at *www.hhs.gov/ocr/hipaa*. You also can do an Internet search on "HIPAA" to find additional resources.

As the medical records are received, the personal injury paralegal will review them to verify the plaintiff's medical history and the injuries and treatment received; to determine if there is any damaging information; to note any additional physicians or facilities from whom to request records; to determine if the plaintiff followed the orders and recommendations of the physicians; and so forth. Make notes regarding the information found and be sure to discuss the same with the supervising attorney. Sometimes the paralegal will be expected to summarize the records either in written or oral form for the attorney. In extremely serious cases, a nurse paralegal or expert may be hired to review and comment on the records.

Unless the attorney instructs otherwise, reports should only be requested from those physicians who are pivotal to the case—in other words, those who treated the plaintiff for injuries resulting from the accident. If there is a preexisting condition, it may be necessary to obtain a report from the primary care physician and/or any specialists who may have treated the plaintiff for that preexisting condition, in order to verify the condition of the plaintiff prior to and after the accident and to document any worsening of the condition since the accident. In the alternative, it may be necessary to prove that the preexisting condition was not adversely affected by the accident or any resulting injuries.

When requesting a report from the treating physician, it is important to ask the physician to describe the injuries sustained, the course of treatment, any permanent damage, and how that damage has affected or will affect the plaintiff and his or her enjoyment of life, including the plaintiff's ability to care for him/herself, work, perform hobbies, and so forth. Ask about the degree or percentage of permanent impairment and any future medical treatment that will be necessary. Be sure also to specifically ask for the diagnosis and prognosis, medications that were prescribed and why, and whether physical therapy was prescribed and completed. Be as thorough as possible in drafting the request to the physician. The physician's records and report are often used by the insurance company in determining whether or not to settle the case (and for how much) and by the attorney to prepare for the physician's deposition, if one is deemed necessary.

As with any other type of litigation, the personal injury paralegal may be asked to summarize depositions taken in the case; draft necessary motions, briefs, and proposed orders; interview witnesses; and perform research related to the case.

Another important task the paralegal performs is to obtain itemized statements from each health care provider, review them to determine the specific charges that relate directly to the case, and create a spreadsheet with a running tally of damages. Other damages that may be included on the spreadsheet include lost or damaged items such as eyeglasses, watch, clothing, and other personal items; medications required as a result of the injuries received; and in some instances, mileage and parking fees for traveling to and from doctor appointments. There may be other expenses that can qualify for reimbursement if incurred as a direct result of the injuries to the plaintiff. For example, if the plaintiff lives alone and has a pet, it may have to be boarded while the plaintiff is hospitalized or is recuperating and is unable to care for the pet. The cost of the boarding may be a reimbursable expense.

Lost wages are another legitimate expense. If a claim for lost wages is made, the paralegal will request proof of the total amount of lost wages. This will require documentation from the employer of such items as the amount of time lost from work and the rate of pay, for example. The paralegal will draft an authorization for release of employment information to be signed by the plaintiff and a letter to the employer setting forth the information required to establish the amount of lost wages. If the plaintiff has disability insurance, the paralegal will obtain information from the insurance carrier regarding the amount of disability payments made and whether the carrier wishes to establish a subrogation claim.

A settlement demand letter is often drafted by the personal injury paralegal, and it usually includes a detailed description of when and how the accident occurred, the injuries sustained, course of treatment, lost wages, loss of consortium, and monetary damages, for example, and then normally leaves a blank for total amount of compensation to be demanded. Depending on the preferences of the attorney and the knowledge and experience of the paralegal, the attorney may or may not request input from the paralegal as to the amount to be demanded, but the attorney will get input from the client before making the final determination. The paralegal will then be responsible for putting together any and all supporting documentation to be included in the settlement demand package.

In some cases, the parties will agree to mediate the case. This may occur prior to or after the filing of a Complaint. In preparation for mediation, the paralegal will gather together the documentation of the injuries and damages, lost wages, and any significant medical records and reports that the mediator may wish to see. The paralegal often drafts the pre-mediation statement. The pre-mediation statement will include much the same information as the settlement demand letter, along with a description of any settlement negotiations to date and the amount that the attorney believes the plaintiff is entitled to receive. At mediation, the paralegal will assist the attorney with exhibits and information needed from the file, provide support to the client, and perform any other duties as requested by the attorney.

At trial, the personal injury paralegal performs many of the same functions as a paralegal would in any other type of litigation, including taking notes, assisting the attorney with exhibits and trial presentations, helping with witnesses, and providing emotional support and information to the client as the case progresses. The paralegal may also assist the attorney during jury selection, draft instructions, and may perform any other necessary functions.

OTHER

There are a multitude of other practice areas. Paralegals work in bankruptcy, collections, criminal defense and prosecution, labor and employment, Social Security disability, elder care, health care, entertainment and sports, and many other areas. There is hardly an area of law in which a paralegal would not be utilized.

Specific knowledge of a practice area is gained over time and through on-the-job experience. It will not happen overnight. By utilizing the foundation established through education, the paralegal builds knowledge and competence by actually working in that area. Remember that, as a paralegal, your first priority is to do your best at whatever it is you are doing. Do not be afraid to ask for help or information when it comes to something you do not know.

CONCLUSION

The skills necessary to be a good paralegal are skills that cross all practice areas. A paralegal must be flexible. Especially in a litigation setting, a paralegal works at the whim of the attorney—in other words, the paralegal must be able to shift gears at a moment's notice to deal with emergencies as they arise. It often occurs that the paralegal's plans for the day are put on the back burner in order to deal with new priorities established by the attorney. In addition, a paralegal must be able to multitask (work on several different projects at one time).

The skills that a paralegal gains in one area of law can easily be utilized in any other area. The ability to analyze a situation and determine what is important is a skill that crosses all practice areas. Knowledge of grammar and the ability to write well and to spell are important whether you are a personal injury or criminal defense paralegal. You must be organized, efficient, and logical and have good time management skills. A paralegal must know how to utilize the existing technology—or at least be able to learn it quickly. And finally, all paralegals must understand their ethical and professional responsibilities.

The paralegal profession is one that is interesting, exciting, challenging, and fulfilling. It is a profession that contributes to the delivery of quality and cost-effective legal services. As a paralegal, everything you do can have an effect on the life of another individual. Consequently, you should always strive to be the best and do your best in whatever area of law you may work.

Appendix A

NATIONAL FEDERATION OF PARALEGAL ASSOCIATIONS, INC.

MODEL CODE OF ETHICS AND PROFESSIONAL RESPONSIBILITY AND GUIDELINES FOR ENFORCEMENT

PREAMBLE

The National Federation of Paralegal Associations, Inc. ("NFPA") is a professional organization comprised of paralegal associations and individual paralegals throughout the United States and Canada. Members of NFPA have varying backgrounds, experiences, education and job responsibilities that reflect the diversity of the paralegal profession. NFPA promotes the growth, development and recognition of the paralegal profession as an integral partner in the delivery of legal services.

In May 1993 NFPA adopted its Model Code of Ethics and Professional Responsibility ("Model Code") to delineate the principles for ethics and conduct to which every paralegal should aspire.

Many paralegal associations throughout the United States have endorsed the concept and content of NFPA's Model Code through the adoption of their own ethical codes. In doing so, paralegals have confirmed the profession's commitment to increase the quality and efficiency of legal services, as well as recognized its responsibilities to the public, the legal community, and colleagues.

Paralegals have recognized, and will continue to recognize, that the profession must continue to evolve to enhance their roles in the delivery of legal services. With increased levels of responsibility comes the need to define and enforce mandatory rules of professional conduct. Enforcement of codes of paralegal conduct is a logical and necessary step to enhance and ensure the confidence of the legal community and the public in the integrity and professional responsibility of paralegals.

In April 1997 NFPA adopted the Model Disciplinary Rules ("Model Rules") to make possible the enforcement of the Canons and Ethical Considerations contained in the NFPA Model Code. A concurrent determination was made that the Model Code of Ethics and Professional Responsibility, formerly aspirational in nature, should be recognized as setting forth the enforceable obligations of all paralegals.

The Model Code and Model Rules offer a framework for professional discipline, either voluntarily or through formal regulatory programs.

§1.   NFPA MODEL DISCIPLINARY RULES AND ETHICAL CONSIDERATIONS

1.1   A PARALEGAL SHALL ACHIEVE AND MAINTAIN A HIGH LEVEL OF COMPETENCE.

Ethical Considerations

EC-1.1 (a)   A paralegal shall achieve competency through education, training, and work experience.

EC-1.1 (b)   A paralegal shall aspire to participate in a minimum of twelve (12) hours of continuing legal education, to include at least one (1) hour of ethics education, every two (2) years in order to remain current on developments in the law.

EC-1.1 (c)   A paralegal shall perform all assignments promptly and efficiently.

1.2   A PARALEGAL SHALL MAINTAIN A HIGH LEVEL OF PERSONAL AND PROFESSIONAL INTEGRITY.

Ethical Considerations

EC-1.2 (a)   A paralegal shall not engage in any ex parte communications involving the courts or any other adjudicatory body in an attempt to exert undue influence or to obtain advantage or the benefit of only one party.

EC-1.2 (b)   A paralegal shall not communicate, or cause another to communicate, with a party the paralegal knows to be represented by a lawyer in a pending matter without the prior consent of the lawyer representing such other party.

EC-1.2 (c)   A paralegal shall ensure that all timekeeping and billing records prepared by the paralegal are thorough, accurate, honest, and complete.

EC-1.2 (d)   A paralegal shall not knowingly engage in fraudulent billing practices. Such practices may include, but are not limited to: inflation of hours billed to a client or employer; misrepresentation of the nature of tasks performed; and/or submission of fraudulent expense and disbursement documentation.

EC-1.2 (e)   A paralegal shall be scrupulous, thorough and honest in the identification and maintenance of all funds, securities, and other assets of a client and shall provide accurate accounting as appropriate.

EC-1.2 (f)   A paralegal shall advise the proper authority of non-confidential knowledge of any dishonest or fraudulent acts by any person pertaining to the handling of the funds, securities or other assets of a client. The authority to whom the report is made shall depend on the nature and circumstances of the possible misconduct, (e.g., ethics committees of law firms, corporations and/or paralegal associations, local or state bar associations, local prosecutors, administrative agencies, etc.). Failure to report such knowledge is in itself misconduct and shall be treated as such under these rules.

1.3   A PARALEGAL SHALL MAINTAIN A HIGH STANDARD OF PROFESSIONAL CONDUCT.

Ethical Considerations

EC-1.3 (a)   A paralegal shall refrain from engaging in any conduct that offends the dignity and decorum of proceedings before a court or other adjudicatory body and shall be respectful of all rules and procedures.

EC-1.3 (b)   A paralegal shall avoid impropriety and the appearance of impropriety and shall not engage in any conduct that would adversely affect his/her fitness to practice. Such conduct may include, but is not limited to: violence, dishonesty, interference with the administration of justice, and/or abuse of a professional position or public office.

EC-1.3 (c)   Should a paralegal's fitness to practice be compromised by physical or mental illness, causing that paralegal to commit an act that is in direct violation of the Model Code/Model Rules and/or the rules and/or laws governing the jurisdiction in which the paralegal practices, that paralegal may be protected from sanction upon review of the nature and circumstances of that illness.

EC-1.3 (d)   A paralegal shall advise the proper authority of non-confidential knowledge of any action of another legal professional that clearly demonstrates fraud, deceit, dishonesty, or misrepresentation. The authority to whom the report is made shall depend on the nature and circumstances of the possible misconduct, (e.g., ethics committees of law firms, corporations and/or paralegal associations, local or state bar associations, local prosecutors, administrative agencies, etc.). Failure to report such knowledge is in itself misconduct and shall be treated as such under these rules.

EC-1.3 (e)   A paralegal shall not knowingly assist any individual with the commission of an act that is in direct violation of the Model Code/Model Rules and/or the rules and/or laws governing the jurisdiction in which the paralegal practices.

EC-1.3 (f)   If a paralegal possesses knowledge of future criminal activity, that knowledge must be reported to the appropriate authority immediately.

1.4   **A PARALEGAL SHALL SERVE THE PUBLIC INTEREST BY CONTRIBUTING TO THE IMPROVEMENT OF THE LEGAL SYSTEM AND DELIVERY OF QUALITY LEGAL SERVICES, INCLUDING PRO BONO PUBLICO SERVICES AND COMMUNITY SERVICE.**

Ethical Considerations

EC-1.4 (a)   A paralegal shall be sensitive to the legal needs of the public and shall promote the development and implementation of programs that address those needs.

EC-1.4 (b)   A paralegal shall support efforts to improve the legal system and access thereto and shall assist in making changes.

EC-1.4 (c)   A paralegal shall support and participate in the delivery of Pro Bono Publico services directed toward implementing and improving access to justice, the law, the legal system or the paralegal and legal professions.

EC-1.4 (d)   A paralegal should aspire annually to contribute twenty-four (24) hours of Pro Bono Publico services under the supervision of an attorney or as authorized by administrative, statutory or court authority to:

  1. persons of limited means; or
  2. charitable, religious, civic, community, governmental and educational organizations in matters that are designed primarily to address the legal needs of persons with limited means; or
  3. individuals, groups or organizations seeking to secure or protect civil rights, civil liberties or public rights.

The twenty-four (24) hours of Pro Bono Publico services contributed annually by a paralegal may consist of such services as detailed in this EC-1.4(d), and/or administrative matters designed to develop and implement the attainment of this aspiration as detailed above in EC-1.4(a) B (c), or any combination of the two.

EC-1.4 (e)   A paralegal should aspire to contribute twenty-four (24) hours of Community Service on an annual basis. For purposes of this EC, "Community Service" shall be defined as: volunteer activities that have the effect of providing a valuable service or benefit to a local community, as distinguished from those services which fall within

© National Federation of Paralegal Associations, Inc. 2006

the traditional definition of *pro bono publico*. By way of example and not limitation, several examples of Community Service may include: working with Habitat for Humanity, volunteering with local women's shelters, volunteering for hurricane relief, serving meals at local soup kitchens or local homeless shelters.

1.5   **A PARALEGAL SHALL PRESERVE ALL CONFIDENTIAL INFORMATION PROVIDED BY THE CLIENT OR ACQUIRED FROM OTHER SOURCES BEFORE, DURING, AND AFTER THE COURSE OF THE PROFESSIONAL RELATIONSHIP.**

Ethical Considerations

EC-1.5 (a)   A paralegal shall be aware of and abide by all legal authority governing confidential information in the jurisdiction in which the paralegal practices.

EC-1.5 (b)   A paralegal shall not use confidential information to the disadvantage of the client.

EC-1.5 (c)   A paralegal shall not use confidential information to the advantage of the paralegal or of a third person.

EC-1.5 (d)   A paralegal may reveal confidential information only after full disclosure and with the client's written consent; or, when required by law or court order; or, when necessary to prevent the client from committing an act that could result in death or serious bodily harm.

EC-1.5 (e)   A paralegal shall keep those individuals responsible for the legal representation of a client fully informed of any confidential information the paralegal may have pertaining to that client.

EC-1.5 (f)   A paralegal shall not engage in any indiscreet communications concerning clients.

1.6   **A PARALEGAL SHALL AVOID CONFLICTS OF INTEREST AND SHALL DISCLOSE ANY POSSIBLE CONFLICT TO THE EMPLOYER OR CLIENT, AS WELL AS TO THE PROSPECTIVE EMPLOYERS OR CLIENTS.**

Ethical Considerations

EC-1.6 (a)   A paralegal shall act within the bounds of the law, solely for the benefit of the client, and shall be free of compromising influences and loyalties. Neither the paralegal's personal or business interest, nor those of other clients or third persons, should compromise the paralegal's professional judgment and loyalty to the client.

EC-1.6 (b)   A paralegal shall avoid conflicts of interest that may arise from previous assignments, whether for a present or past employer or client.

EC-1.6 (c)   A paralegal shall avoid conflicts of interest that may arise from family relationships and from personal and business interests.

EC-1.6 (d)   In order to be able to determine whether an actual or potential conflict of interest exists a paralegal shall create and maintain an effective recordkeeping system that identifies clients, matters, and parties with which the paralegal has worked.

EC-1.6 (e)   A paralegal shall reveal sufficient non-confidential information about a client or former client to reasonably ascertain if an actual or potential conflict of interest exists.

EC-1.6 (f)   A paralegal shall not participate in or conduct work on any matter where a conflict of interest has been identified.

EC-1.6 (g)   In matters where a conflict of interest has been identified and the client consents to continued representation, a paralegal shall comply fully with the implementation and maintenance of an Ethical Wall.

1.7   A PARALEGAL'S TITLE SHALL BE FULLY DISCLOSED.

Ethical Considerations

EC-1.7 (a)   A paralegal's title shall clearly indicate the individual's status and shall be disclosed in all business and professional communications to avoid misunderstandings and misconceptions about the paralegal's role and responsibilities.

EC-1.7 (b)   A paralegal's title shall be included if the paralegal's name appears on business cards, letterhead, brochures, directories, and advertisements.

EC-1.7 (c)   A paralegal shall not use letterhead, business cards or other promotional materials to create a fraudulent impression of his/her status or ability to practice in the jurisdiction in which the paralegal practices.

EC-1.7 (d)   A paralegal shall not practice under color of any record, diploma, or certificate that has been illegally or fraudulently obtained or issued or which is misrepresentative in any way.

EC1.7 (e)   A paralegal shall not participate in the creation, issuance, or dissemination of fraudulent records, diplomas, or certificates.

1.8   A PARALEGAL SHALL NOT ENGAGE IN THE UNAUTHORIZED PRACTICE OF LAW.

Ethical Considerations

EC-1.8 (a)   A paralegal shall comply with the applicable legal authority governing the unauthorized practice of law in the jurisdiction in which the paralegal practices.

§2.   NFPA GUIDELINES FOR THE ENFORCEMENT OF THE MODEL CODE OF ETHICS AND PROFESSIONAL RESPONSIBILITY

2.1   BASIS FOR DISCIPLINE

2.1(a)   Disciplinary investigations and proceedings brought under authority of the Rules shall be conducted in accord with obligations imposed on the paralegal professional by the Model Code of Ethics and Professional Responsibility.

2.2   STRUCTURE OF DISCIPLINARY COMMITTEE

2.2(a)   The Disciplinary Committee ("Committee") shall be made up of nine (9) members including the Chair.

2.2(b)   Each member of the Committee, including any temporary replacement members, shall have demonstrated working knowledge of ethics/professional responsibility-related issues and activities.

2.2(c)   The Committee shall represent a cross-section of practice areas and work experience. The following recommendations are made regarding the members of the Committee.
   1. At least one paralegal with one to three years of law-related work experience.
   2. At least one paralegal with five to seven years of law related work experience.

3. At least one paralegal with over ten years of law related work experience.
4. One paralegal educator with five to seven years of work experience; preferably in the area of ethics/professional responsibility.
5. One paralegal manager.
6. One lawyer with five to seven years of law-related work experience.
7. One lay member.

2.2(d) The Chair of the Committee shall be appointed within thirty (30) days of its members' induction. The Chair shall have no fewer than ten (10) years of law-related work experience.

2.2(e) The terms of all members of the Committee shall be staggered. Of those members initially appointed, a simple majority plus one shall be appointed to a term of one year, and the remaining members shall be appointed to a term of two years. Thereafter, all members of the Committee shall be appointed to terms of two years.

2.2(f) If for any reason the terms of a majority of the Committee will expire at the same time, members may be appointed to terms of one year to maintain continuity of the Committee.

2.2(g) The Committee shall organize from its members a three-tiered structure to investigate, prosecute and/or adjudicate charges of misconduct. The members shall be rotated among the tiers.

2.3   OPERATION OF COMMITTEE

2.3(a) The Committee shall meet on an as-needed basis to discuss, investigate, and/or adjudicate alleged violations of the Model Code/ Model Rules.

2.3(b) A majority of the members of the Committee present at a meeting shall constitute a quorum.

2.3(c) A Recording Secretary shall be designated to maintain complete and accurate minutes of all Committee meetings. All such minutes shall be kept confidential until a decision has been made that the matter will be set for hearing as set forth in Section 6.1 below.

2.3(d) If any member of the Committee has a conflict of interest with the Charging Party, the Responding Party, or the allegations of misconduct, that member shall not take part in any hearing or deliberations concerning those allegations. If the absence of that member creates a lack of a quorum for the Committee, then a temporary replacement for the member shall be appointed.

2.3(e)   Either the Charging Party or the Responding Party may request that, for good cause shown, any member of the Committee not participate in a hearing or deliberation. All such requests shall be honored. If the absence of a Committee member under those circumstances creates a lack of a quorum for the Committee, then a temporary replacement for that member shall be appointed.

2.3(f)   All discussions and correspondence of the Committee shall be kept confidential until a decision has been made that the matter will be set for hearing as set forth in Section 6.1 below.

2.3(g)   All correspondence from the Committee to the Responding Party regarding any charge of misconduct and any decisions made regarding the charge shall be mailed certified mail, return receipt requested, to the Responding Party's last known address and shall be clearly marked with a "Confidential" designation.

2.4   PROCEDURE FOR THE REPORTING OF ALLEGED VIOLATIONS OF THE MODEL CODE/DISCIPLINARY RULES

2.4(a)   An individual or entity in possession of non-confidential knowledge or information concerning possible instances of misconduct shall make a confidential written report to the Committee within thirty (30) days of obtaining same. This report shall include all details of the alleged misconduct.

2.4(b)   The Committee so notified shall inform the Responding Party of the allegation(s) of misconduct no later than ten (10) business days after receiving the confidential written report from the Charging Party.

2.4(c)   Notification to the Responding Party shall include the identity of the Charging Party, unless, for good cause shown, the Charging Party requests anonymity.

2.4(d)   The Responding Party shall reply to the allegations within ten (10) business days of notification.

2.5   **PROCEDURE FOR THE INVESTIGATION OF A CHARGE**
                 OF MISCONDUCT

2.5(a)   Upon receipt of a Charge of Misconduct ("Charge"), or on its own
                 initiative, the Committee shall initiate an investigation.

2.5(b)   If, upon initial or preliminary review, the Committee makes a
                 determination that the charges are either without basis in fact
                 or, if proven, would not constitute professional misconduct, the
                 Committee shall dismiss the allegations of misconduct. If such
                 determination of dismissal cannot be made, a formal investigation
                 shall be initiated.

2.5(c)   Upon the decision to conduct a formal investigation, the Committee
                 shall:

1. mail to the Charging and Responding Parties within
   three (3) business days of that decision notice of the
   commencement of a formal investigation. That notification shall be in writing and shall contain a complete
   explanation of all Charge(s), as well as the reasons for a
   formal investigation and shall cite the applicable codes
   and rules;

2. allow the Responding Party thirty (30) days to prepare
   and submit a confidential response to the Committee,
   which response shall address each charge specifically
   and shall be in writing; and

3. upon receipt of the response to the notification, have
   thirty (30) days to investigate the Charge(s). If an extension of time is deemed necessary, that extension shall
   not exceed ninety (90) days.

2.5(d)   Upon conclusion of the investigation, the Committee may:

1. dismiss the Charge upon the finding that it has no basis
   in fact;

2. dismiss the Charge upon the finding that, if proven, the
   Charge would not constitute Misconduct;

3. refer the matter for hearing by the Tribunal; or

4. in the case of criminal activity, refer the Charge(s)
   and all investigation results to the appropriate
   authority.

2.6   PROCEDURE FOR A MISCONDUCT HEARING BEFORE A TRIBUNAL

2.6(a)   Upon the decision by the Committee that a matter should be heard, all parties shall be notified and a hearing date shall be set. The hearing shall take place no more than thirty (30) days from the conclusion of the formal investigation.

2.6(b)   The Responding Party shall have the right to counsel. The parties and the Tribunal shall have the right to call any witnesses and introduce any documentation that they believe will lead to the fair and reasonable resolution of the matter.

2.6(c)   Upon completion of the hearing, the Tribunal shall deliberate and present a written decision to the parties in accordance with procedures as set forth by the Tribunal.

2.6(d)   Notice of the decision of the Tribunal shall be appropriately published.

2.7   SANCTIONS

2.7(a)   Upon a finding of the Tribunal that misconduct has occurred, any of the following sanctions, or others as may be deemed appropriate, may be imposed upon the Responding Party, either singularly or in combination:

1. letter of reprimand to the Responding Party; counseling;
2. attendance at an ethics course approved by the Tribunal; probation;
3. suspension of license/authority to practice; revocation of license/authority to practice;
4. imposition of a fine; assessment of costs; or
5. in the instance of criminal activity, referral to the appropriate authority.

2.7(b)   Upon the expiration of any period of probation, suspension, or revocation, the Responding Party may make application for reinstatement. With the application for reinstatement, the Responding Party must show proof of having complied with all aspects of the sanctions imposed by the Tribunal.

2.8 APPELLATE PROCEDURES

2.8(a)   The parties shall have the right to appeal the decision of the Tribunal in accordance with the procedure as set forth by the Tribunal.

DEFINITIONS

"Appellate Body" means a body established to adjudicate an appeal to any decision made by a Tribunal or other decision-making body with respect to formally-heard Charges of Misconduct.

"Charge of Misconduct" means a written submission by any individual or entity to an ethics committee, paralegal association, bar association, law enforcement agency, judicial body, government agency, or other appropriate body or entity, that sets forth non-confidential information regarding any instance of alleged misconduct by an individual paralegal or paralegal entity.

"Charging Party" means any individual or entity who submits a Charge of Misconduct against an individual paralegal or paralegal entity.

"Competency" means the demonstration of: diligence, education, skill, and mental, emotional, and physical fitness reasonably necessary for the performance of paralegal services.

"Confidential Information" means information relating to a client, whatever its source, that is not public knowledge nor available to the public. ("Non-Confidential Information" would generally include the name of the client and the identity of the matter for which the paralegal provided services.)

"Disciplinary Hearing" means the confidential proceeding conducted by a committee or other designated body or entity concerning any instance of alleged misconduct by an individual paralegal or paralegal entity.

"Disciplinary Committee" means any committee that has been established by an entity such as a paralegal association, bar association, judicial body, or government agency to: (a) identify, define and investigate general ethical considerations and concerns with respect to paralegal practice; (b) administer and enforce the Model Code and Model Rules and; (c) discipline any individual paralegal or paralegal entity found to be in violation of same.

"Disclose" means communication of information reasonably sufficient to permit identification of the significance of the matter in question.

"Ethical Wall" means the screening method implemented in order to protect a client from a conflict of interest. An Ethical Wall generally includes, but is not limited to, the following elements: (1) prohibit the paralegal from having any connection with the matter; (2) ban discussions with or the transfer of documents to or from the paralegal; (3) restrict access to files; and (4) educate all members of the firm, corporation, or entity as to the separation of the paralegal (both organizationally and physically) from the pending matter. For more information regarding the Ethical Wall, see the NFPA publication entitled "The Ethical Wall — Its Application to Paralegals."

"Ex parte" means actions or communications conducted at the instance and for the benefit of one party only, and without notice to, or contestation by, any person adversely interested.

"Investigation" means the investigation of any charge(s) of misconduct filed against an individual paralegal or paralegal entity by a Committee.

"Letter of Reprimand" means a written notice of formal censure or severe reproof administered to an individual paralegal or paralegal entity for unethical or improper conduct.

"Misconduct" means the knowing or unknowing commission of an act that is in direct violation of those Canons and Ethical Considerations of any and all applicable codes and/or rules of conduct.

"Paralegal" is synonymous with "Legal Assistant" and is defined as a person qualified through education, training, or work experience to perform substantive legal work that requires knowledge of legal concepts and is customarily, but not exclusively performed by a lawyer. This person may be retained or employed by a lawyer, law office, governmental agency, or other entity or may be authorized by administrative, statutory, or court authority to perform this work.

"Pro Bono Publico" means providing or assisting to provide quality legal services in order to enhance access to justice for persons of limited means; charitable, religious, civic, community, governmental and educational organizations in matters that are designed primarily to address the legal needs of persons with limited means; or individuals, groups or organizations seeking to secure or protect civil rights, civil liberties or public rights.

"Proper Authority" means the local paralegal association, the local or state bar association, Committee(s) of the local paralegal or bar association(s), local prosecutor, administrative agency, or other tribunal empowered to investigate or act upon an instance of alleged misconduct.

"Responding Party" means an individual paralegal or paralegal entity against whom a Charge of Misconduct has been submitted.

"Revocation" means the recision of the license, certificate or other authority to practice of an individual paralegal or paralegal entity found in violation of those Canons and Ethical Considerations of any and all applicable codes and/or rules of conduct.

"Suspension" means the suspension of the license, certificate or other authority to practice of an individual paralegal or paralegal entity found in violation of those Canons and Ethical Considerations of any and all applicable codes and/or rules of conduct.

"Tribunal" means the body designated to adjudicate allegations of misconduct.

Appendix B

(Sample)

PETITION FOR DISSOLUTION OF MARRIAGE

[Husband/Wife/Petitioner/Respondent], being first duly sworn, says:

1. He/She is the Husband/Wife of
2. He/She resides at ___ and has been a resident of ____ County for more than ____ (__) months last past and a resident of the State of _____ for more than ___ (__) months last past and [Husband/Wife/Petitioner/Respondent] resides at __.
3. The parties were married on the __ day of __, ____, and separated on or about the _____ day of _____, ____.

4. The parties acquired certain property and incurred certain obligations during the course of their marriage and a reasonable division thereof should be made.

5. The marriage of the parties is irretrievably broken.

6. There were no children born of this marriage and Wife is not now pregnant.

WHEREFORE, [Husband/Wife/Petitioner/Respondent] prays that his/her marriage to [Husband/Wife/Petitioner/Respondent] be dissolved; and that

1. The Court make an equitable division of the property of the parties.

2. An order be entered restoring Wife's former name of ___;

3. [Husband/Wife/Petitioner/Respondent] be order to pay the cost of this action;

4. For all other just and proper relief.

I affirm under the penalties for perjury that the above representations are true to the best of my knowledge, information and belief.

_____

SUBSCRIBED AND SWORN to before me, a Notary Public, in and for said County and State, this _____ day of _____, ____.

My Commission Expires:

_____
Notary Public,_____

_____
Resident of _____ County

DOE LAW FIRM

By_____

State Bar No.
Attorneys for

(caption)

(Sample)

PETITION FOR DISSOLUTION OF MARRIAGE, FOR PROVISIONAL ORDERS AND AFFIDAVIT IN SUPPORT THEREOF

[Husband/Wife/Petitioner/Respondent], being first duly sworn, says:

1. He/She is the Husband/Wife of ____.
2. He/She resides at __ and has been a resident of ___ County for more than ___ (__) months last past and a resident of the State of ____ for more than __ (__) months last past and Husband/Wife resides at _____.
3. The parties were married on the___ day of ___, ____, and separated on or about the _____ day of _____, ____.
4. The parties acquired certain property and incurred certain obligations during the course of their marriage and a reasonable division thereof should be made.
5. The marriage of the parties is irretrievably broken.
6. There were no children born of this marriage and Wife is not now pregnant.

   OR

6. The children born of this marriage are emancipated and Wife is not now pregnant.

   OR

6. The parties are the parents of ____ ( ) minor children whose names and birth dates are ___, born ____; and ____, born ___.
7. The present address of the minor children of the parties is ___, and that said children reside with [Husband/Wife/Petitioner/Respondent].
8. [Husband/Wife/Petitioner/Respondent] has not participated in any other litigation concerning the custody of said children in this or any other state.
9. [Husband/Wife/Petitioner/Respondent] has no information of any custody proceeding concerning the children in a court in Indiana or in any other state.

10. No person not a party to this proceeding has physical custody of the children or claims to have custody or visitation rights with respect to said children.

11. [Husband/Wife/Petitioner/Respondent] is a fit and proper person to be awarded the custody of the children of the parties.

    OR

11. [Husband and Wife/Petitioner and Respondent] are fit and proper persons to be awarded the joint custody of the children of the parties.

12. [Husband/Wife/Petitioner/Respondent] has in the past _____ and [Husband/Wife/Petitioner/Respondent] requests that a Protective Order be entered, after hearing, restraining both parties from molesting, harassing, disturbing the peace of or committing an assault or battery upon the other party.

13. There is a danger that [Husband/Wife/Petitioner/Respondent] will conceal, transfer, destroy, encumber, or dispose of the property or incur debts in the joint names of the parties. Therefore, [Husband/Wife/Petitioner/Respondent] requests that a Joint [Preliminary Injunction/Restraining Order] be entered, after hearing, restraining both parties from transferring, encumbering, concealing, selling or otherwise disposing of any joint property of the parties or asset of the marriage except in the normal course of business or for the necessities of life, without the written consent of the parties or the permission of the Court.

    OR

13. In order to preserve the marital estate, [Husband/Wife/Petitioner/Respondent] requests that a [Joint Preliminary Injunction/Restraining Order] be entered, after hearing, restraining both parties from transferring, encumbering, concealing, selling or otherwise disposing of any joint property of the parties or asset of the marriage except in the normal course of business or for the necessities of life, without the written consent of the parties or the permission of the Court.

14. In order to preserve the Court's jurisdiction over the minor children of the parties, the [Husband/Wife/Petitioner/Respondent] requests that a [Joint Preliminary Injunction/Restraining Order] be entered, after hearing, restraining both parties from removing the minor children of

the parties then residing in the State of Indiana from the State with the intent to deprive this Court of jurisdiction over such children without the prior written consent of all parties or the permission of the Court.

15. [Husband/Wife/Petitioner/Respondent] is without sufficient money, means or property by which to pay her/his attorney fees.

16. [Husband/Wife/Petitioner/Respondent] is incapacitated to the extent that his/her ability to support herself/himself is materially affected and he/she requires maintenance from [Husband/Wife/Petitioner/Respondent].

17. ___ interrupted or postponed education, training, or employment during the marriage as a result of homemaking or child care responsibilities or both and ___ therefore requires rehabilitative maintenance from ___.

18. [Husband/Wife/Petitioner/Respondent] is without sufficient means to support herself/himself and the children of the parties during the pendency of this action.

19. [Husband/Wife/Petitioner/Respondent] moves the Court for an order scheduling this matter for preliminary hearing and believes that it will require approximately _____ hours/minutes of the Court's time.

20. [Husband/Wife/Petitioner/Respondent] moves the Court for the entry of a [Joint Preliminary Injunction/Restraining Order], after hearing, restraining the parties from:

   a. Concealing, transferring, destroying, encumbering, selling or otherwise disposing of any joint property of the parties or assets of the marriage except in the normal course of business or for the necessities of life, without the written consent of the parties or the permission of the Court.

   b. Incurring debts in the joint names of the parties.

   c. Removing the minor children of the parties then residing in the State of Indiana from the State with the intent to deprive this Court of jurisdiction over such children without the prior written consent of all parties or the permission of the Court.

   d. Interfering with each party's temporary possession of their respective personal property and effects.

   e. Interfering with use of the automobile presently in each party's possession.

   f. Changing the insured parties or beneficiaries on any life, health, casualty, liability, or annuity policies.

21. [Husband/Wife/Petitioner/Respondent] moves the Court for the entry of a Protective Order, after hearing, restraining the _____ from:
    a. Molesting, harassing, disturbing the peace of or committing or threatening to commit an assault or battery upon the ___.
    b. Residing at, approaching, entering or coming about the residence of the ___.
    c. Bothering or molesting the ___ at any time or place.
    d. Bothering or harassing the ___ at his/her place of business and from approaching, entering or coming about the place of business of ___.
    e. Approaching, entering or coming about the premises occupied by ___.
22. [Husband/Wife/Petitioner/Respondent] moves the Court for a provisional order, after hearing, as follows:
    a. [Husband/Wife/Petitioner/Respondent] shall have temporary custody of the minor children of the parties.
    b. [Husband/Wife/Petitioner/Respondent] shall have temporary possession of certain property, namely, ___.
    c. [Husband/Wife/Petitioner/Respondent] shall support [Husband/Wife/Petitioner/Respondent] and the minor children pending final hearing.
    d. [Husband/Wife/Petitioner/Respondent] shall pay preliminary fees for the services of [Husband/Wife/Petitioner/Respondent]'s attorneys.
    e. [Husband/Wife/Petitioner/Respondent] be restrained from interfering with [Husband/Wife/Petitioner/Respondent]'s temporary possession of __.
    f. [Husband/Wife/Petitioner/Respondent] be restrained from residing at, approaching, entering, or coming about the residence of the parties located at _____ (add any other provisions).
    g. That the [Joint Preliminary Injunction/Restraining Order] be made permanent.

WHEREFORE, [Husband/Wife/Petitioner/Respondent] prays that his/her marriage to ___ be dissolved; and that
1. [Husband/Wife/Petitioner/Respondent] be granted the care and custody of the minor children of the parties;

2. A reasonable sum be ordered from [Husband/Wife/Petitioner/Respondent] for the support of said minor children.

3. The Court make an equitable division of the property of the parties.

4. [Husband/Wife/Petitioner/Respondent] be ordered to make maintenance payments to [Husband/Wife/Petitioner/Respondent];

5. [Husband/Wife/Petitioner/Respondent] be ordered to pay rehabilitative maintenance to [Husband/Wife/Petitioner/Respondent];

6. An order for preliminary and final fees for the services of [Husband/Wife/Petitioner/Respondent]'s attorney be entered;

7. An order be entered restoring Wife's former name of ____;

8. [Husband/Wife/Petitioner/Respondent] be order to pay the cost of this action;

9. For all other just and proper relief.

I affirm under the penalties for perjury that the above representations are true to the best of my knowledge.

_____

SUBSCRIBED AND SWORN to before me, a Notary Public, in and for said County and State, this _____ day of _____, 2000.

_____

DOE LAW FIRM

By_____

State Bar No.
Attorneys for

A.	HOUSEHOLD FURNISHINGS/ FURNITURE/ELECTRONIC EQUIPMENT/APPLIANCES	GROSS VALUE	DEBT	NET VALUE	H	W	J
	1.	In Husband's Possession						
	2.	In Wife's Possession						
B.	VEHICLES—boats/RVs/cycles (make/model/year)						
	3.			0.00	0.00			
	4.			0.00	0.00			
	5.			0.00	0.00			
	6.			0.00	0.00			
	7.							
C.	CASH/ACCOUNTS/CDs (name of bank account, last four digits of account number/ account type)						
	8.			0.00	0.00			
	9.			0.00	0.00			
	10.			0.00	0.00			
	11.			0.00	0.00			
	12.			0.00	0.00			
	13.			0.00	0.00			
	14.			0.00	0.00			
D.	SECURITIES/STOCKS/BONDS						
	15.			0.00	0.00			
	16.			0.00	0.00			
	17.			0.00	0.00			
	18.			0.00	0.00			
E.	REAL ESTATE (including mobile homes)	FMV	MORTGAGE	NET FMV			
	19.	Marital Residence (address)						
		First Mortgagor:						
		Second Mortgagor:						
	20.	Other Residence (address)						
		First Mortgagor:						
		Second Mortgagor:						

		DEFERRED COMPENSATION—profit sharing, pension plans, Keoghs, IRAs, 401(k)s, SEP	% VESTED	VESTED FMV	H	W	J
F.							
	21.						
	22.						
	23.						
	24.						
	25.						
	26.						
	27.						
	28.						
G.		BUSINESS INTERESTS	% interest	% FMV	H	W	J
	29.						
	30.						
H.		LIFE INSURANCE—term and group	Face Amount	Policy No.	Beneficiary	H	W	J
	31.							
	32.							
	33.							
I.		LIFE INSURANCE—whole	Cash Value	Loan Amt.	% interest	H	W	J
	34.							
	35.							
	36.							
J.		OTHER ASSETS—collections/ jewelry/antiques/silver/china/ art/cameras	Value	Debt	Net Value	H	W	J
	37.				0.00			
	38.				0.00			
	39.				0.00			
	40.				0.00			
	41.				0.00			
	42.				0.00			
	43.				0.00			

List names, ages, and relationships of persons living in your household:

_____

_____

Are other persons in your household working? _____

If so, who? _____

Occupation:_____ Employer: _____

I declare under penalties for perjury that the foregoing, including any attachment(s), is true and correct to the best of my knowledge and belief.

Signature: _____

Printed Name: _____

Dated: _____

You are under a duty to supplement or amend this Financial Declaration prior to hearing if you learn the information provided is incorrect or the information provided is no longer true.

Prepared by:

_____

Firm Name _____

Firm Address _____

_____

Phone _____

X v. Y

CAUSE NO.

Date of Marriage: _____

Date of Filing: _____

Valuation Date: _____

Last revised: _____

Summary of Marital Estate and Proposed Distribution

Assets and Debts	Asset Value	Debt	Net Equity	To Wife	To Husband	Source for Value
Marital Residence: 123 Any Lane Street, Anytown, IN						
First Mortgage: AnyBank USA	$ 250,000.00	123,299.44	373,299.44	186,649.72	186,649.72	Appraisal, mortgage statement
John Doe Mortgage Co—2nd mortgage-marital residence		(53,451.23)	(53,451.23)	(53,451.23)		Mortgage statement
Other Real Estate:						
Lake Cottage	$ 200,000.00	0.00	200,000.00		200,000.00	Appraisal
250 Acres—Montana (W inheritance)	$1,000,000.00	0.00	1,000,000.00	1,000,000.00		Appraisal
Household goods & furnishings	$ 15,000.00	0.00	15,000.00	7,500.00	7,500.00	Appraisal
Husband's tools	$ 30,000.00	0.00	30,000.00		30,000.00	Appraisal
Wife's jewelry	$ 9,500.00	0.00	9,500.00	9,500.00		Appraisal
Vehicles:						
2008 Chevrolet Silverado 1500 4WD	$ 33,500.00	0.00	33,500.00		33,500.00	H Ans to Interrog #13
2007 Lexus RX 350	$ 34,170.00	(13,782.15)	20,387.85	20,387.85		estimated value per online source
2002 Jeep Wrangler SE Sport	$ 9,625.00	0.00	9,625.00		9,625.00	Estimated value per online source
2005 Ski Boat	$ 10,000.00	0.00	10,000.00		10,000.00	H Ans to Interrog #13
2006 Pontoon	$ 15,500.00	0.00	15,500.00		15,500.00	H Ans to Interrog #13

(continued)

Summary of Marital Estate and Proposed Distribution *(continued)*

Assets and Debts	Asset Value	Debt	Net Equity	To Wife	To Husband	Source for Value
Bank Accounts:						
Big Bank USA checking #2259	$ 3,523.11		3,523.11		3,523.11	Ans to Interrog #10
Big Bank USA savings #2260	$ 33,298.45		33,298.45		33,298.45	Ans to Interrog #10
Big Bank USA savings #2261	$ 10,238.95		10,238.95	10,238.95		Ans to Interrog #10
Big Bank USA money market #2262	$ 5,259.00		45,259.00	22,629.50	22,629.50	Ans to Interrog #10
Stocks, Bonds, Securities:						
Microsoft Corporation—25 shares	$ 697.75	0.00	697.75		697.75	W Ans to Interrog #11
Exxon Mobil Corp.—355 shares	$ 30,253.10	0.00	30,253.10		30,253.10	W Ans to Interrog #11
Retirement Accounts:						
ExxonMobil 401(k) fund (H)	$ 249,223.97	0.00	249,223.97		249,223.97	Statement
Pension (H)	$ 57,370.67		57,370.67		57,370.67	Valuation
IRA #1 (W)	$ 85,299.60		85,299.60	5,299.60		W Ans to Interrog #17
IRA #2 (W)	$ 94,922.14		94,922.14	94,922.14		W Ans to Interrog #17
Debts:						
Student loan (H)		($9,653.51)	(9,653.51)		(9,653.51)	Statement
VISA credit card		($1,559.08)	(1,559.08)		(1,559.08)	Statement
Other credit card		($1,809.94)	(1,809.94)		(1,809.94)	Statement
Total Marital Estate	$2,217,381.74	43,043.53	2,260,425.27	1,383,676.53	876,748.74	
Net Marital Estate:			2,260,425.27			
Percentage of Net Marital Estate:				61.21%	38.79%	

(caption)

(*Sample Dissolution of Marriage*)

INTERROGATORIES TO RESPONDENT/PETITIONER

Comes now the Respondent/Petitioner, by counsel, and propounds the following Interrogatories to the Respondent/Petitioner to be answered hereinbelow by said Respondent/Petitioner, under oath, in writing, and within thirty (30) days hereof.

Interrogatories

1. State your full name, current address, date of birth, and social security number.

ANSWER:

2. State your occupation and place of employment or whether you are self-employed and the name of your business or businesses, including the address for each such place of employment or business.

ANSWER:

3. For each employer, business, or businesses referred to in interrogatory number 2, state the following information:
   A. Your present position;
   B. Your average number of hours per week worked in the last year; and,
   C. How often you are paid;

ANSWER:

4. For each pay period, state:
   A. Gross Pay;
   B. Average bonus, commission, overtime, and other pay in addition to base pay;
   C. Net Pay;
   D. Specify each deduction by name and amount withheld;
   E. The number of deductions you claim on your W-4 form; and
   F. Identify all benefits which you receive as a result of your employment, including but not limited to health insurance, life insurance, thrift and savings plan, profit sharing, savings or pension plan, bonds of any kind.

ANSWER:

5. Please identify by name of fund and identification number every pension fund, Keogh plan, retirement fund, individual retirement account, annuity fund, or any other similar benefit plans or funds, including military benefits, or any program entitling you to deferred compensation, in which you have any interest.

ANSWER:

6. For each of said funds identified in the preceding interrogatory, please state:
   A. Whether said fund is contributory or non-contributory;
   B. The amount you may receive from said fund upon demand;
   C. The amount you may receive from said fund upon termination of your employment;
   D. The retirement ages contemplated by said plans;
   E. The benefits available at retirement both in monthly installments and/or lump sum payment;
   F. The present value of said fund and the method used to calculate same;

ANSWER:

7. For each of the funds referred to in the preceding interrogatories, please state whether each is vested at the present time and give all factors supporting your conclusion.

ANSWER:

8. For any fund referred to in the preceding interrogatories which is not vested, please state when such fund will become vested and all factors supporting your conclusion that the fund is not vested.

ANSWER:

9. Please state all contributions since ___, to each of the funds referred to in the preceding interrogatories indicating the dates, amounts, and contributions of each.

ANSWER:

10. Do you receive any other monies, income, wages, commissions or profits, including, but not limited to rents, dividends and contract rights?

ANSWER:

11. If the answer to the foregoing question is "Yes", state separately for each source of monies, income, wages, commissions, or profits:
    A. The amount received;
    B. The nature of such payments;
    C. The source; and
    D. The total amount received by you since _____.

ANSWER:

12. Describe fully all bank accounts, certificates of savings, certificates of deposit, Christmas club accounts, savings accounts, savings bonds, corporate or municipal bonds, notes receivable, flexible stockbroker accounts, accounts receivable, checking accounts and trust funds which you owned (or own) alone or with other persons, or in the name of your children, since the date of your marriage to Petitioner/Respondent, including but not limited to the following details:
    a. The amount of each at the time of filing this action;
    b. The present balance;
    c. The bank or other institution where such item is located or the person, firm or corporation who is obligated thereby to pay you, and the address;
    d. The rate of interest applicable to such item;
    e. The exact name which appears on the account, certificate, trust, or note as the owner, beneficiary or payee, as the case may be;
    f. The date such account or trust was created or the date the note was acquired;
    g. The account number; and
    h. The persons having custody of the records concerning the account.

ANSWER:

13. State the name of any financial institutions to whom you have furnished a credit application or a financial statement since ____.

ANSWER:

14. Describe fully all life insurance policies or annuity contracts which you own alone or with any other person, including, but not limited to the following details:
    a. Face value;
    b. Present cash surrender value;
    c. The cash surrender value on the date of filing this action;
    d. The policy or contract number;
    e. The name and address of the company which issued such policy or contract;
    f. The amount and frequency of payments to be received by you under such policy or contract;
    g. The name and address of the designated beneficiary or person entitled to the proceeds thereof;
    h. Whether any loans have been made against said policy or contract; and if so, for each loan, state: the original amount; the date taken out; the purpose, the name of the person making each payment, the balance owed on the date of filing and the balance owed as of the present date.

ANSWER:

15. With respect to all real estate owned by you alone or with any other person or in which you have any legal or equitable interest, state the following details:
    a. The address or legal description of the property;
    b. The exact names and addresses of the legal owners;
    c. The date acquired;
    d. The purchase price;

    e. The sale price, if sold;

    f. Whether or not the same is subject to a contract for sale and if so, the terms of each contract;

    g. The unpaid principal balance of any mortgage, and the name and address of the mortgagee, on the date of filing; and,

    h. The unpaid principal balance of any mortgage, and the name and address of the mortgagee, as of the present date;

    i. The name and address of the person, firm or corporation in possession thereof;

    j. The amount of rent received;

    k. Whether or not the same is subject to a written lease and, if so, the terms of each lease;

    l. Your opinion as to the current fair market value, if you have such an opinion;

    m. Your opinion as to the fair market value as of the date of filing; and,

    n. The nature of any interest therein formerly held by the Petitioner and now extinguished, together with an explanation of how such interest ceased to be.

ANSWER:

16. State the amount of cash in your possession or subject to your control and the location thereof.

ANSWER:

17. Describe by model, make and year each vehicle of transportation, including but not limited to automobiles, trucks, boats, airplanes and motorcycles, owned by you alone or jointly with any other person and, with respect to each vehicle of transportation, the following details:

    a. The name or names appearing on any certificate of title to the vehicle;

b. The date acquired;

c. The purchase price;

d. The name and address of any lienholder;

e. The unpaid principal balance of any indebtedness thereon on the date of filing;

f. The unpaid principal balance of any indebtedness thereon as of the present date; and,

g. Your opinion as to the current fair market value, if you have such an opinion.

ANSWER:

18. Describe fully all other personal property owned by you alone or jointly with other persons, having a value of $1,000 or more, including but not limited to the following details:

a. Date acquired;

b. Purchase price;

c. The name and address of co-owner, if any; and

d. Present location of the item.

ANSWER:

19. Identify each stock, stock option, bond or other security of any foreign or domestic corporation, company, or firm in which you maintain any ownership interest. Also state:

a. The name of each security;

b. The date purchased;

c. The purchase price;

d. The present physical location of such security;

e. The name and address of any joint or co-owner; and

f. The fair market value of each on the date of filing this action; and,

g. The present value and how you arrived at that value.

ANSWER:

20. For each transfer or sale of securities during the last two (2) years, state:
    a. The name and number of securities transferred;
    b. The date of each sale or transfer;
    c. The sale of transfer price of each security;
    d. The name and address of each broker through whom such transfer was effected;
    e. The cost basis for each security transferred; and
    g. The net gain or loss resulting from each such transfer.

ANSWER:

21. Are there any safe deposit boxes, vaults, safes, or other places of deposit and safe-keeping in which you deposited and money, documents or other items of personal property from the date of your marriage to the Respondent to the present date? If so, for each place of deposit, state:
    a. The name and address of depository institution or other place of deposit;
    b. The number or other means of identification of deposits;
    c. The name and address of each person authorized to enter the deposit;
    d. The date the deposit was commenced;
    e. The date the deposit was terminated; and
    f. State the contents of said box on the date of filing this action; and,
    g. State the contents of said box at the present time.

ANSWER:

22. Does any person, firm or business hold any funds or property for your benefit in a trust or otherwise? If so, identify with specificity the property, its value, the date and amount of each distribution of income or corpus to you, and the name and address of the trustee.

ANSWER:

23. Are you holding any property for the benefit of another person in trust or otherwise? If so, for each item of property, state:
   a. The name and address of the beneficial owner;
   b. A description of the property;
   c. The value of the property;
   d. The authority under which you are holding it; and
   e. The condition or terms under which it is held.

ANSWER:

24. For each loan or debt which you currently have, please state as follows:
   a. To whom the obligation is owed;
   b. The collateral, if any, when you took out the loan or incurred said debt;
   c. Specifically, how you used the proceeds of the loan or why the debt was incurred;
   d. Is anyone other than yourself obligated on the loan, and if so, who;
   e. The original loan amount;
   f. The balance owed on the date of filing;
   g. The current balance owed;
   h. State the amount per month you pay towards said loan; and
   i. State the date on which the loan or debt becomes due.

ANSWER:

25. State whether you have any unpaid income tax due and owing the Federal government, the State of ____, or any municipality. If so, describe in detail.

ANSWER:

26. Since the date of your marriage to Petitioner/Respondent, have you received any property by bequest, devise, descent, or as a gift?

ANSWER:

27. If so, for each item of property or funds received, state:
    a. Date of receipt;
    b. Description of property received;
    c. Value of property when received;
    d. Value of property on the date of filing;
    e. Present value of your interest in the property;
    f. Present location of the property;
    g. Name of the estate;
    h. Name and address of the executor or administrator of the estate;
    i. Title and address of the court administering the estate; and
    j. File or cause number of the estate in the court records.

ANSWER:

28. State all items of property which you will ask the Court to award to Petitioner/Respondent. State all items of property which you will ask the Court to award to you.

ANSWER:

29. Do you contend (or will you argue) that an unequal division of the marital estate is just and reasonable? If so, state the facts upon which you will rely for your argument.

ANSWER:

30. Do you contend that one party made a significantly greater or lesser contribution to the acquisition of the marital property of the parties? If so, specifically describe the type of contribution.

ANSWER:

31. List all liabilities which you will ask the Court to order Wife to assume. List all liabilities you will ask the Court to order Husband to assume. For each such liability, list: to whom the liability is owed and the amount owed as of the date of responding to these interrogatories.

ANSWER:

32. State with specificity all other orders which you will ask the Court to make, including but not limited to payment of attorney's fees, payment of maintenance or support, and reimbursement by either Wife or Husband to the other of any expenses incurred.

ANSWER:

33. Please describe with specificity all documents you have removed from the marital residence that you believe are in any way relevant to the issues in this proceeding and the present location of such documents, including, without limitation, any correspondence to which either you or your spouse is a party.

ANSWER:

34. Please describe with specificity the monies you removed from the parties= joint accounts, both personal and business, including the current location of said monies, name of bank, account number, etc., and provide a complete accounting of all such funds, and state the current balance remaining.

ANSWER:

35. Please list the name, address, and telephone number of each witness you intend to call at the final hearing of this matter, including a brief description of the testimony you expect from said witness.

ANSWER:

I affirm, under the penalties for perjury, that the foregoing answers to interrogatories are true and complete to the best of my information.

Dated:_____   _____

                                          __ [*insert name*]

Please take notice that a copy of the answers must be served on the undersigned within thirty (30) days after the service of these interrogatories.

The foregoing interrogatories are to be regarded as a continuing and you are requested to provide, by way of supplemental answers thereto, such additional information as may hereafter be obtained by you or your counsel, or any person on your behalf, which will augment or otherwise modify any answers now given to the foregoing interrogatories. Such supplemental responses are to be filed and served upon the Petitioner's/Respondent's attorney within thirty (30) days after receipt of such information, but not later than the time of the trial.

Respectfully submitted,
DOE LAW FIRM

(caption)

(*Sample Dissolution*)

REQUEST FOR PRODUCTION OF DOCUMENTS
TO RESPONDENT/PETITIONER

Comes now the Petitioner/Respondent, by counsel, and pursuant to Trial Rule _____ of the _____(*insert state*) Rules of Trial Procedure, requests the Respondent/Petitioner to produce the following designated documents, within thirty (30) days of the receipt hereof.

Requests

1. Copies of your last six (6) pay stubs.

RESPONSE:

2. Copies of Federal and State income tax returns, and all accompanying forms and schedules, including W-2s for the years _____.

RESPONSE:

3. Copies of all personal bank account statements and checkbook registers from _____ to date.

RESPONSE:

4. Copies of any and all employment contracts to which you are a party.

RESPONSE:

5. Copies of all accounts statements received from brokerage houses, corporations, mutual funds, etc., showing dividends paid to you from January 1, _____ to date.

RESPONSE:

6. Copies of all accounts statements received by you regarding pension fund, Keogh plan, retirement fund, individual retirement account, annuity fund, or any other similar benefit plans or funds, including military benefits, or any program entitling you to deferred compensation, in which you have any interest from January 1, _____ to date.

RESPONSE:

7. Copies of all decrees (or like orders of Court) showing distribution to you from any decedent's estate in the 12-months immediately preceding your response to this request for production.

RESPONSE:

8. Copies of trust instruments of which you are a beneficiary.

RESPONSE:

9. A copy of the closing statement(s) for the sale of any real estate in which you had any equitable or legal interest since _____

RESPONSE:

10. A copy of the purchase Agreement(s) for any real estate purchased by or for you since _____

RESPONSE:

11. A copy of any existing leasehold agreement(s) and/or sub-leasehold agreement(s) relating to any apartment(s) or real estate owned by you.

RESPONSE:

12. Copies of Purchase Agreements relating to real estate in which you presently have a legal or equitable interest <u>other</u> than that mentioned in Interrogatory No. ___.

RESPONSE:

13. Copies of all Buy-Sell Agreements to which you are a party.

RESPONSE:

14. Copies of all purchase agreements relating to any business or business enterprise in which you presently have an interest.

RESPONSE:

15. Please attach hereto a copy of your completed ____ County Courts Financial Declaration.

RESPONSE:

16. Copies of any and all documents used in answering or which support the figures listed in your Financial Declaration requested in item number ____ above.

RESPONSE:

17. Copies of any and all journals or diaries or other notes you have kept in which there is any reference to the Petitioner/Respondent or the children since ___

RESPONSE:

18. Copies of all documents described in, used in answering, and/or in support of, your answer to Interrogatory Number ____.

RESPONSE:

19. True, complete and authentic copies of all exhibits you intend to introduce at the final hearing of this matter.

RESPONSE:

Please take notice that a copy of your Response must be served on the undersigned within thirty (30) days after the service of these Requests.

The foregoing requests are to be regarded as a continuing and you are requested to provide, by way of supplemental response thereto, such additional information as may hereafter be obtained by you or your counsel, or any person on your behalf, which will augment or otherwise modify any responses now given to the foregoing requests for production. Such supplemental responses are to be filed and served upon the Respondent's attorney within thirty (30) days after receipt of such information, but not later than the time of the trial.

Respectfully submitted,

DOE LAW FIRM

Issued by the

UNITED STATES DISTRICT COURT

V.

SUBPOENA IN A CIVIL CASE

Case Number:[1]

TO:

☐ YOU ARE COMMANDED to appear in the United States District court at the place, date, and time specified below to testify in the above case.

PLACE OF TESTIMONY	COURTROOM
	DATE AND TIME

☐ YOU ARE COMMANDED to appear at the place, date, and time specified below to testify at the taking of a deposition in the above case.

PLACE OF DEPOSITION	DATE AND TIME

☐ YOU ARE COMMANDED to produce and permit inspection and copying of the following documents or objects at the place, date, and time specified below (list documents or objects):

PLACE	DATE AND TIME

☐ YOU ARE COMMANDED to permit inspection of the following premises at the date and time specified below.

PREMISES	DATE AND TIME

     Any organization not a party to this suit that is subpoenaed for the taking of a deposition shall designate one or more officers, directors, or managing agents, or other persons who consent to testify on its behalf, and may set forth, for each person designated, the matters on which the person will testify. Federal Rule of Civil Procedure 30(b)(6).

ISSUING OFFICER'S SIGNATURE AND TITLE (INDICATE IF ATTORNEY FOR PLAINTIFF OR DEFENDANT)	DATE

ISSUING OFFICER'S NAME, ADDRESS AND PHONE NUMBER

(See Federal Rule of Civil Procedure 45 (c), (d), and (e), on next page)

[1] If action is pending in district other than district of issuance, state district under case number.

AO88 (Rev. 12/07) Subpoena in a Civil Case (Page 2)

PROOF OF SERVICE

	DATE	PLACE
SERVED		

SERVED ON (PRINT NAME)	MANNER OF SERVICE

SERVED BY (PRINT NAME)	TITLE

DECLARATION OF SERVER

I declare under penalty of perjury under the laws of the United States of America that the foregoing information contained in the Proof of Service is true and correct.

Executed on _____

DATE	SIGNATURE OF SERVER
	ADDRESS OF SERVER

Federal Rule of Civil Procedure 45 (c), (d), and (e), as amended on December 1, 2007:

(c) PROTECTING A PERSON SUBJECT TO A SUBPOENA.

(1) Avoiding Undue Burden or Expense; Sanctions. A party or attorney responsible for issuing and serving a subpoena must take reasonable steps to avoid imposing undue burden or expense on a person subject to the subpoena. The issuing court must enforce this duty and impose an appropriate sanction — which may include lost earnings and reasonable attorney's fees — on a party or attorney who fails to comply.

(2) Command to Produce Materials or Permit Inspection.

(A) Appearance Not Required. A person commanded to produce documents, electronically stored information, or tangible things, or to permit the inspection of premises, need not appear in person at the place of production or inspection unless also commanded to appear for a deposition, hearing, or trial.

(B) Objections. A person commanded to produce documents or tangible things or to permit inspection may serve on the party or attorney designated in the subpoena a written objection to inspecting, copying, testing or sampling any or all of the materials or to inspecting the premises — or to producing electronically stored information in the form or forms requested. The objection must be served before the earlier of the time specified for compliance or 14 days after the subpoena is served. If an objection is made, the following rules apply:

(i) At any time, on notice to the commanded person, the serving party may move the issuing court for an order compelling production or inspection.

(ii) These acts may be required only as directed in the order, and the order must protect a person who is neither a party nor a party's officer from significant expense resulting from compliance.

(3) Quashing or Modifying a Subpoena.

(A) When Required. On timely motion, the issuing court must quash or modify a subpoena that:

(i) fails to allow a reasonable time to comply;

(ii) requires a person who is neither a party nor a party's officer to travel more than 100 miles from where that person resides, is employed, or regularly transacts business in person — except that, subject to Rule 45(c)(3)(B)(iii), the person may be commanded to attend a trial by traveling from any such place within the state where the trial is held;

(iii) requires disclosure of privileged or other protected matter, if no exception or waiver applies; or

(iv) subjects a person to undue burden.

(B) When Permitted. To protect a person subject to or affected by a subpoena, the issuing court may, on motion, quash or modify the subpoena if it requires:

(i) disclosing a trade secret or other confidential research, development, or commercial information;

(ii) disclosing an unretained expert's opinion or information that does not describe specific occurrences in dispute and results from the expert's study that was not requested by a party; or

(iii) a person who is neither a party nor a party's officer to incur substantial expense to travel more than 100 miles to attend trial

(C) Specifying Conditions as an Alternative. In the circumstances described in Rule 45(c)(3)(B), the court may, instead of quashing or modifying a subpoena, order appearance or production under specified conditions if the serving party:

(i) shows a substantial need for the testimony or material that cannot be otherwise met without undue hardship; and

(ii) ensures that the subpoenaed person will be reasonably compensated.

(d) DUTIES IN RESPONDING TO A SUBPOENA.

(1) Producing Documents or Electronically Stored Information. These procedures apply to producing documents or electronically stored information:

(A) Documents. A person responding to a subpoena to produce documents must produce them as they are kept in the ordinary course of business or must organize and label them to correspond to the categories in the demand.

(B) Form for Producing Electronically Stored Information Not Specified. If a subpoena does not specify a form for producing electronically stored information, the person responding must produce it in a form or forms in which it is ordinarily maintained or in a reasonably usable form or forms.

(C) Electronically Stored Information Produced in Only One Form. The person responding need not produce the same electronically stored information in more than one form.

(D) Inaccessible Electronically Stored Information. The person responding need not provide discovery of electronically stored information from sources that the person identifies as not reasonably accessible because of undue burden or cost. On motion to compel discovery or for a protective order, the person responding must show that the information is not reasonably accessible because of undue burden or cost. If that showing is made, the court may nonetheless order discovery from such sources if the requesting party shows good cause, considering the limitations of Rule 26(b)(2)(C). The court may specify conditions for the discovery.

(2) Claiming Privilege or Protection.

(A) Information Withheld. A person withholding subpoenaed information under a claim that it is privileged or subject to protection as trial-preparation material must:

(i) expressly make the claim; and

(ii) describe the nature of the withheld documents, communications, or tangible things in a manner that, without revealing information itself privileged or protected, will enable the parties to assess the claim.

(B) Information Produced. If information produced in response to a subpoena is subject to a claim of privilege or of protection as trial-preparation material, the person making the claim may notify any party that received the information of the claim and the basis for it. After being notified, a party must promptly return, sequester, or destroy the specified information and any copies it has; must not use or disclose the information until the claim is resolved; must take reasonable steps to retrieve the information if the party disclosed it before being notified; and may promptly present the information to the court under seal for a determination of the claim. The person who produced the information must preserve the information until the claim is resolved.

(e) CONTEMPT.

The issuing court may hold in contempt a person who, having been served, fails without adequate excuse to obey the subpoena. A nonparty's failure to obey must be excused if the subpoena purports to require the nonparty to attend or produce at a place outside the limits of Rule 45(c)(3)(A)(ii).

AO 440 (Rev. 04/08)　Civil Summons

UNITED STATES DISTRICT COURT
for the

_____)
　　　　　　　Plaintiff　　　　　　　　)
　　　　　　　　v.　　　　　　　　　　　)　　Civil Action No.
_____)
　　　　　　　Defendant　　　　　　　　)

Summons in a Civil Action

To: _(Defendant's name and address)_

A lawsuit has been filed against you.

　　　　Within ___ days after service of this summons on you (not counting the day you received it), you must serve on the plaintiff an answer to the attached complaint or a motion under Rule 12 of the Federal Rules of Civil Procedure. The answer or motion must be served on the plaintiff's attorney, whose name and address are:

If you fail to do so, judgment by default will be entered against you for the relief demanded in the complaint. You also must file your answer or motion with the court at 46 East Ohio Street, Room 105, Indianapolis, IN 46204.

　　　　　　　　　　　　　　　　　　　　_____
　　　　　　　　　　　　　　　　　　　　　　　　　Name of clerk of court

Date: _____　　　　_____
　　　　　　　　　　　　　　　　　　　　　　　　　Deputy clerk's signature

(Use 60 days if the defendant is the United States or a United States agency, or is an officer or employee of the United States allowed 60 days by Rule 12(a)(3).)

✎ AO 440 (Rev. 04/08) Civil Summons (Page 2)

Proof of Service

I declare under penalty of perjury that I served the summons and complaint in this case on _____,
by:

    (1) personally delivering a copy of each to the individual at this place, _____
_____ ; or

    (2) leaving a copy of each at the individual's dwelling or usual place of abode with _____
who resides there and is of suitable age and discretion; or

    (3) delivering a copy of each to an agent authorized by appointment or by law to receive it whose name is
_____ ; or

    (4) returning the summons unexecuted to the court clerk on _____; or

    (5) other *(specify, i.e. certified mail)* _____
_____
_____ .

My fees are \$ _____ for travel and \$ _____ for services, for a total of \$ _0.00_ .

Date: _____

_____
Server's signature

_____
Printed name and title

_____
Server's address

In addition to preparing a case management plan, counsel shall prepare a case management plan summary to submit to the court. The purpose of the summary is to provide the court with a simple, in-chambers reference regarding the case. The summary must fit on one page and include the following information in the following format:

MAGISTRATE JUDGE'S SUMMARY OF CASE MANAGEMENT PLAN

Date Approved: (for court's use)   **Cause No.**:

Caption:

Pltf's Counsel: (include name and telephone number)

Deft's Counsel: (include name and telephone number)

Nature of Case: (state nature of claim (e.g. tort, breach of contract, employment discrimination (gender), etc.) and SHORT factual synopsis)

Defenses: (state SHORT factual synopsis and summary of defenses)

Discovery: Completed by (date in CMP)

Readiness: Trial in (month and year in CMP)

Trial Time: ___ days (also include whether trial by jury or to the court)

Motions Pending: (list any motions currently pending)

Motions Future: Amend pleadings/add parties by ___; summary judgment by _____ (dates in CMP)

Pltf's Demand: Due (date in CMP)   **Defense Offer**: Due (date in CMP)

Settlement: Court settlement conference/private mediation (select one)

Remarks: (for court's use)

The use of unambiguous abbreviations is encouraged. A sample summary is attached for your reference.

MAGISTRATE JUDGE'S SUMMARY OF CASE MANAGEMENT PLAN

Date Approved: **Cause No.**: 1:02-CV-4562 LJM/WTL

Caption: John Smith v. Jane Doe, Inc.

Pltf's Counsel: Peter Piper: 555-1111

Deft's Counsel: Snow White: 555-2222

Nature of Case: Breach of implied warranty of merchantability; pltf purchased a briefcase
                            manufactured by deft; handles on briefcase broke, briefcase opened, and
                            pltf's very important papers flew out into traffic and were ruined

Defenses: Pltf misused briefcase by filling it too full; briefcase was merchantable
                            and would not have broken otherwise

Discovery: Complete **12-1-03**

Readiness: Trial in **February 2004**

Trial Time: 3 days by jury

Motions Pending: None

Motions Future: Amend pleadings/add parties by **8-1-03**; summary judgment by **11-20-03**

Pltf's Demand: Due **10-1-03**   **Defense Offer**: +15 days

Settlement: Parties request a settlement conf. with the M.J. in approx. 3 mnths

Remarks:

INSTRUCTIONS TO DEPONENT

1. *Listen to the question*

Concentrate on every word. Wait until you hear the last word of the question before you start your answer. If you listen closely to ordinary conversation, you will see that we cut one another off quite frequently, not to be rude, but to keep the conversation moving. Listening is hard work. If you listen as you should, you will be able to state a concise, appropriate response.

2. *Be sure you hear the question*

If the lawyer drops his voice or someone coughs and you miss a word or two, say that you did not hear the question. Do this even if you are almost certain that you know what word you missed.

3. *Be sure you understand the question*

Sometimes the question will be so long or so convoluted that you do not know what you are being asked except that it concerns subject A. You may be tempted to answer by saying something about subject A in the hope that the lawyer will then go on to some other subject. Do not do that. Just say that you do not understand.

You may not understand because the lawyer is not exact in his language. For example, he may ask you if a certain letter was sent after "that." You may not be sure to what fact or event he is referring when he says "that." Say that you do not understand the question.

If you do not understand, do not help the other lawyer in asking the question. Do not say, "If you mean this, then my answer would be such and such; if you mean that, my answer would be so and so." You may very well give the other lawyer ideas. Say only that you do not understand.

4. *Answer the question*

After you have listened to, heard, and understood the question, then answer the question. Generally you should keep your answer short and to the point.

What you learned in taking tests in school applies here. Answer what you are asked. If the question begins "Who," your answer should be a name; if "Where," a place; if "When," a date; and so on.

If you do not know or do not remember, say that. Do not guess. If you are estimating or approximating, say that you are.

Sometimes, after you give your answer there will be a silence. The other lawyer may be thinking how to word his next question. Silences sometimes make a witness uncomfortable. You may be tempted to fill the silence with words. Do not do that. Keep quiet and wait.

If a question irritates you or makes you angry, resist the temptation to argue with the other lawyer, you will lose. Just give whatever facts you know responsive to the question and then keep quiet.

If you are asked a question that requires a longer answer, give it. Use your common sense. But if you are in doubt, keep your answer short. Do not make speeches. Remember that every word is another target for the other lawyer.

In dealing with the other lawyer, your manner should be courteous and open, but mentally you should be on guard at all times. Even if something is said "off the record," the other lawyer can ask you about it when you are back on the record.

I may object to certain questions. Try not to be distracted by that. Listen to the objection. It may point out some hidden trap in the question. The objection is a reminder to you to keep concentrating.

I may go further and instruct you not to answer the question. If I do, follow my instruction.

5. *Stick to truthful answers*

You may hear the same question more than once. If your original answer was accurate, stick to it. The fact that the other lawyer keeps coming back to the question does not mean that you are not answering properly. You must give the facts as you know them. If you gave them right the first time, stick to your answer.

Assume the other lawyer is an experienced and skillful questioner. Through his questions he may try to create doubt in your mind even about facts that you know very well. Take an easy example which has nothing to do with this case. Suppose he shows you a coffee cup and asks you what it is. You say a coffee cup. He then pauses, gazes at the cup, and lets you squirm. Then, after letting you wonder what he knows that you don't, he leans forward and says, "Now, Mr. Witness, is it your testimony here today under oath that that object is a coffee cup? Do you really mean to say that?" There is a natural tendency to back off and say, "Well, I thought it was a coffee cup." That small change in your testimony may be crucial. Suppose a witness says the first time that he had the green light and then says that he thought he had it. That would be a devastating change. So if your first answer was true, stick to it and say, "Yes, it is a coffee cup." What does the other lawyer do then? He will then go on to another subject quickly when he sees that you cannot be shaken.

Of course, if you realize that your earlier answer was in error or incomplete, you should correct or supplement it. Obviously, you should not say that an earlier answer is true if you become aware that it is not.

6. *Tell the truth*

You must always follow that rule. You should not interpret anything else that I have said to you to be at odds with that rule.

7. *What to expect of me*

I will ask a few questions, perhaps, but only if I think clarification of your testimony is important. Again, listen to the question, because I will probably want you to clarify or improve on your earlier testimony.

Other than these general rules, I think it is important for you to organize your thought process to make certain that your recollection is as complete as possible and that the order of events or the approximate chronology is in mind.

If you have any questions on these thoughts, please don't hesitate to give me a call. Thank you.

SAMPLE INTERROGATORIES TO COMPANY DEFENDANT IN PERSONAL INJURY (AUTO COLLISION) CASE

PLAINTIFFS' INTERROGATORIES TO
DEFENDANT _____

Come now the Plaintiffs by counsel, and pursuant to Trial Rule ____ of the _____ Rules of Procedure, request that the Defendant _____ answer the following Interrogatories fully, in writing and under oath, and return to the offices of _____, within thirty (30) days of service hereof.

DEFINITIONS

"You", "your", and "yourself" shall include the Defendants and other persons acting or purporting to act on behalf of the Defendant including any agent, attorney, or other representative of the Defendant.

"Subject incident", "subject collision", and "collision" shall refer to the motor vehicle collision which occurred on [date] in _____ County, [State] which is the subject of this lawsuit.

"Driver" or "your driver" shall refer to the driver of your vehicle at the time of the subject incident.

INTERROGATORIES

1. Please identify yourself, giving your full name, residence address, business address, title or office with Defendant, educational background, length of time you have been employed by Defendant, your basic job description with Defendant at the time of the subject incident and now.

ANSWER:

2. Prior to answering these Interrogatories, have you made a full and complete investigation of all facts known to your company with the intent of answering these Interrogatories with all the available information?

ANSWER:

3. State the name and address of the owner of the vehicle involved in the collision that occurred on [date] at [location] in _____ County, [State], which collision is referred to in Plaintiff's Complaint and described herein as the "subject incident".

ANSWER:

4. At the time of the subject incident, were you the named insured on any policies of liability insurance?

ANSWER:

5. If the answer to the foregoing question is "yes" the following with respect to each of such policies of liability insurance:
   (a) The name and address of the company issuing such policy;
   (b) The number of such policy;
   (c) The limits of liability of such policy;
   (d) The named insured under such policy;
   (e) The vehicle, or vehicles, in connection with which such policy was issued;
   (f) The nature and extent of the coverage which protects your company and/or your employee, agent or servant against risks such as this suit.

ANSWER:

6. Was the vehicle involved in the subject incident owned or leased by the Defendant at the time of this incident? Please explain in detail.

ANSWER:

7. Is the full legal name of the Defendant correctly d in the Complaint? If not, what is the full and correct legal name of the Defendant?

ANSWER:

8. Was an employee, agent, or servant of yours involved in a motor vehicle collision that occurred on [date] at [location] in _____ County, [State], and, if so, his or her name, address and telephone number and whether you conducted an investigation into said incident.

ANSWER:

9. State the full name, address, telephone number and business capacity of every person in your motor vehicle at the time of the subject collision.

ANSWER:

10. If you conducted an investigation, please the nature of the investigation, which employee or representative of your company conducted the same, and who is in possession of the investigation file, witness ments, photographs, or any other documentary evidence related thereto.

ANSWER:

11. Do you know of any witnesses, other than the Plaintiff and Defendant, to the subject collision? If so, please give their full name, address, and telephone number.

ANSWER:

12. Please give the names, addresses, and telephone numbers of all persons to whom oral or other ments were made regarding the subject collision, including when and where such ments were made, and who is in possession of such ments.

ANSWER:

13. Give your version of a full description of how the collision occurred, including at least the following information:
    (a) The exact time of the occurrence;
    (b) The place of the occurrence;
    (c) The direction of travel of the Plaintiff's vehicle at the time of the collision;
    (d) Plaintiff's physical location immediately prior to the collision;
    (e) Your employee, agent, or servant's direction of travel and physical location immediately prior to the collision;
    (f) The Plaintiff's actions at and just before the time of the incident;
    (g) Your employee, agent, or servant's actions at and just before the time of the incident;
    (h) The name of the person you feel was the primary cause of this collision;
    (i) The source of your information.

ANSWER:

14. What, if anything, was done by your employee, agent, or servant in the operation of his motor vehicle in an attempt to avoid the collision?

ANSWER:

I AFFIRM UNDER THE PENALTIES FOR PERJURY, THAT THE FOREGO-ING REPRESENTATION(S) ARE TRUE.

_____

[Name of person signing]

SAMPLE INTERROGATORIES TO INDIVIDUAL DEFENDANT IN PERSONAL INJURY (AUTO COLLISION) CASE

PLAINTIFF'S FIRST SET OF INTERROGATORIES TO DEFENDANT _____

Comes now the Plaintiff by counsel, and pursuant to Trial Rule _____ of the [State} Rules of Procedure, request that the Defendant _____ answer the following Interrogatories fully, in writing, and under oath, and return those answers to the offices of _____, within thirty (30) days of service hereof.

DEFINITIONS

"You", "your", and "yourself" shall mean [Defendant] or other persons acting or purporting to act on behalf of the Defendant including any agent, attorney or other representative of the Defendant.

"Subject incident", "subject collision", and "collision" shall refer to the collision which occurred on [date] at [location] in _____ County, [State] which is the subject of this lawsuit.

INTERROGATORIES

1. State your:
   (a) Full name;
   (b) Home address;
   (c) Home telephone number;
   (d) Business address;
   (e) Business telephone number;
   (f) Date of Birth;
   (g) Social Security number;
   (h) Driver's License number;
   (i) Marital status at time of incident & spouse's name;
   (j) Current marital status & spouse's name;

ANSWER:

2. Was the vehicle involved in the subject incident owned or leased by the Defendant? Please explain in detail.

ANSWER:

3. Were you employed at the time of the subject incident? If so, by whom?

ANSWER:

4. At the time of the collision were you serving any employer? If so, please explain in detail.

ANSWER:

5. At the time of the collision were you acting in the course and scope of your employment? If so, please explain in detail.

ANSWER:

6. With reference to your driving history state;
    (a) Any citations you may have received in the last ten years;
    (b) The disposition of each;
    (c) The penalty or fine imposed;
    (d) The nature of any restrictions;
    (e) The reason for any restrictions;
    (f) Any action taken by your employer.

ANSWER:

7. With reference to the trip you were making at the time of the subject incident herein, please state:
    (a) Where it started;
    (b) When it started;
    (c) Where it was scheduled to end;
    (d) When you were scheduled to arrive at your intended destination;
    (e) The stops which you made prior to the collision;
    (f) The stops which you intended to make over the uncompleted part of your trip;
    (g) The reason, or reasons, for the trip;
    (h) The number of miles you had already traveled at the time of the incident.

ANSWER:

8. Was there anything distracting you, interfering with your driving, impeding you, or bothering you at or just before the time of the collision? If so, explain in detail.

ANSWER:

9. Can you give any estimate of the speed of any of the vehicles involved in, or in a position to observe, the subject collision at anytime before, leading up to, and at the time of the collision. If so, please provide all such estimates for each vehicle.

ANSWER:

10. Describe the:
    (a) Weather;
    (b) Visibility; and
    (c) Condition of roadway;

ANSWER:

11. Describe in detail all recollections that you have regarding the events leading up to the subject collision, the collision itself, and the events following the collision, beginning with the first things you recall occurring on the morning of the collision, including all observations of the vehicles involved, and ending with the last thing you recall on the evening of the collision.

ANSWER:

12. State in detail everything you did to avoid the subject collision.

ANSWER:

13. Did you consider swerving your motor vehicle or putting on your brakes sooner than you actually did? If so, please fully explain.

ANSWER:

14. Is there anything you could have done to avoid the collision which you did not do? If so, explain in detail.

ANSWER:

15. Describe the path of travel of each vehicle after the collision until it came to a final resting place.

ANSWER:

16. At the time of the collision in question, what was the condition of the brakes, signaling devices, tires and steering apparatus of your vehicle?

ANSWER:

17. At the time of the collision in question, did you know, or do you now know, of any mechanical, operational, or other problem with the vehicle you were driving? If so, describe fully.

ANSWER:

18. Do you contend that the Plaintiffs violated any traffic law at the time of, or immediately prior to, the collision in question? If so, please describe by statute or number, or generally what you contend to be such traffic violation.

ANSWER:

19. Describe any information you have indicating, or any reason you have to believe, that there was any defect in the road or in the marking or signing on the road that caused or contributed to cause the collision in question.

ANSWER:

20. Describe any information you have which leads you to believe, or upon which you base any contention, that weather or any weather condition was a factor or contributed to this collision in any way.

ANSWER:

21. Were there any obstructions to visibility for any of the operators of any of the vehicles involved in this incident at the time of, or immediately before, the collision in question which you contend was a factor or contributed to cause the collision in question? If so, please fully describe.

ANSWER:

22. Do you allege, or do you intend to allege, that someone else's conduct was the "proximate cause" of the collision in question? If so, describe in detail such other alleged cause.

ANSWER:

23. Describe in detail what damage was done to your vehicle, and give the cost of repair to your vehicle.

ANSWER:

24. Describe in detail what injuries, if any, you received in the collision.

ANSWER:

25. Were you ever admitted to any hospital or other medical facility for the treatment of any illness, injury or condition resulting from the collision? If so, for each hospitalization state
    (a) The name and address of the hospital or facility;
    (b) The date of the hospitalization or treatment;
    (c) Describe in detail the reasons for your confinement.

ANSWER:

26. State in detail what drugs or medication, if any, you had taken during the 24 hour period before the subject incident.

ANSWER:

27. In the 24 hour period before the subject incident, did you have anything of an alcoholic and/or intoxicating nature to drink? If so, state;
    (a) The name, type, and brand of each drink consumed;
    (b) That quantity consumed;
    (c) The name and address of each place of consumption;
    (d) The exact time of consumption of each drink;
    (e) The name, type and brand of each drink given to any other person present at the time of your consumption.

ANSWER:

28. Describe in detail what you did the evening and night before the subject incident. Where did you spend the night? With whom did you spend the evening and night?

ANSWER:

29. At the time of the incident, did you own a pair of eyeglasses or other corrective lenses? If so, were you wearing them at the time of the incident?

ANSWER:

30. State the speed of your vehicle at all times material to the subject incident, including specifically your speed at, and just before, the time of impact, and if your brakes were on at the time of impact please state your speed before applying your brakes.

ANSWER:

31. Please state whether or not you know of or have a copy of any statement which the Plaintiffs or others have previously made concerning the subject incident. If so, please attach.

ANSWER:

32. Describe in detail any comments or statements you heard or any conversation you had with the Plaintiffs or witnesses following the collision in question.

ANSWER:

33. Identify, by name, address and telephone number, each person known to you, your attorney, or anyone acting on your behalf who has any knowledge regarding the facts and circumstances surrounding the subject incident, and/or the events leading up to the subject incident.

ANSWER:

34. Prior to the collision herein, had you been involved in any collisions involving motor vehicles? If so, as to each, state:
    (a) The date, time, and location of the collision;
    (b) The names and addresses of the driver involved;
    (c) If legal proceedings were commenced the court in which they were filed and the cause number;
    (d) The names of parties and status they occupied in any action;
    (e) The result of any judgment rendered in any action;
    (f) The result of any settlement in absence of legal proceedings;
    (g) The nature of all vehicles or instrumentalities involved;
    (h) The nature and extent of any injuries that you sustained.

ANSWER:

35 Were you charged by the city, county, or state with the violation of any traffic regulation as a result of the operation of your motor vehicle at or just prior to the occurrence of the subject incident? If so, state:
    (a) The charge,
    (b) The plea entered.
    (c) The final disposition.

ANSWER:

36 Have you ever been convicted of any criminal offense, including traffic offenses, unrelated to the subject incident? If so, for each conviction, state:
    (a) The date on which the offense was committed.
    (b) The date of conviction.
    (c) The name or type of crime committed.
    (d) The judgment of the court as to the fine and/or imprisonment.
    (e) The name of the city and location of the court in which you were convicted.

ANSWER:

37. Describe any insurance agreement under which any insurance company may be liable to satisfy part or all of the judgment which may be entered in this action, or to indemnify or reimburse for payments made to satisfy the judgment, by stating the name of the insurer, the address, the policy number, and the amount of any liability insurance coverage.

ANSWER:

38. Have you ever been involved in any other lawsuit, either as a Plaintiff or Defendant? If so, please do the following with respect to each lawsuit:
    (a) Identify each occurrence or transaction that gave rise to each lawsuit;
    (b) Describe in detail the nature of the lawsuit, giving the court and cause number;
    (c) Identify the parties and their attorneys of record;
    (d) Describe in detail the injuries and the damages which were sought in such lawsuit; and
    (e) Describe in detail the manner in which it was resolved.

ANSWER:

39. Identify all documents that were referred to in answering these Interrogatories.

ANSWER:

   I AFFIRM UNDER THE PENALTIES FOR PERJURY, THAT THE FOREGOING REPRESENTATION(S) ARE TRUE.

   _____

SAMPLE REQUEST FOR PRODUCTION TO DEFENDANT IN PERSONAL INJURY (AUTO COLLISION) CASE

PLAINTIFFS' REQUEST FOR PRODUCTION TO DEFENDANT _____

Come now the Plaintiffs by counsel, and pursuant to Trial Rule _____ of the [State] Rules of Procedure, request that the Defendant _____ respond fully to the following Request for Production, and return to the offices of _____ within thirty (30) days of service hereof.

DEFINITIONS

FOR THE PURPOSES OF THIS REQUEST FOR PRODUCTION OF DOCUMENTS, THE TERMS USED HEREIN SHALL HAVE THE FOLLOWING MEANINGS:

A. "Document" and "documents" shall be used in their broadest sense and shall mean and include all written, printed, typed, recorded, or graphic matter of every kind and description, both originals and copies, and all attachments and appendices thereto. Without limiting the foregoing, the terms "document" and "documents" shall include all agreements, contracts, communications, correspondence, letters, telegrams, telexes, messages, memoranda, records, reports, books, summaries or other records of personal conversations of interviews, summaries or other records of meetings and conferences, summaries or other records of negotiations, other summaries, diaries, diary entries, calendars, appointment books, time records, instructions, work assignments, visitor records, forecasts, statistical data, statistical statements, financial statements, work sheets, work papers, drafts, graphs, maps, charts, tables, accounts, analytical records, consultants, reports, notices, marginal notations, notebooks, telephone bills or records, bills, statements, records of obligation and expenditure, invoices, lists, journals, advertising, recommendations, files, printouts, compilations, tabulations, purchase orders, receipts, sell orders, confirmations, checks, canceled checks, letters of sell orders, letters of credit, envelopes or folders or similar containers, voucher analyses, studies, surveys, transcripts of hearings, transcripts of testimony, expense reports, microfilm, microfiche, articles, speeches, tape or disc recordings, sound recordings, video recordings, film, tapes, photographs, punch cards, programs, data compilations from which information can be obtained (including matter used in data processing), and other printed, written, handwritten, typewritten, recorded, stenographic, computer-generated, computer-stored, or electronically-stored matter, however and by whomever produced, prepared, reproduced, disseminated, or made. The terms "document" and "documents" shall include all copies of documents by whatever means made, except that where a document is identified or produced, identical copies thereof which do not contain any markings, additions, or deletions different from the original need not be separately produced. Without limiting the term "control", a document is deemed to be within your control if you have ownership, possession or custody of the document, or the right to secure the document or copy thereof from any person or public or private entity having physical possession thereof.

B. "You" and "your" shall mean other persons acting or purporting to act in behalf of including any agent, attorney or other representative.

C. As used herein, the words "and" and "or" shall be construed either conjunctively or disjunctively as required by the context to bring within the scope of these requests any document that might be deemed outside its scope by another construction.

D. "Person" shall mean any individual, partnership, association, corporation, joint venture, firm, proprietorship, agency board, authority, commission, or other legal or business entity.

E. "Communication" shall mean and include every manner or means of disclosure, transfer, or exchange, and every disclosure, transfer, or exchange of information, whether orally or by document or whether face-to-face, by telephone, mail, personal delivery, or otherwise.

F. "Statement" means and includes any written or graphic statement signed or otherwise adopted or approved by the users in making it, any stenographic, mechanical, electric or other recording or transcription thereof which is a substantially verbatim recital of an oral statement made by the person making it and contemporaneously recorded.

G. "Identify" means, in the case of:
   (1) an individual person, to state the person's name, address, telephone number, occupation or profession, job title and the name, address and telephone number of that person's employer;

(2) an organization (e.g., a corporation, partnership or association), to state the organization's name, the type of organization, its address and telephone number, the state in which it is organized (e.g., incorporated) and the identity of its chief executive;

(3) a document, to state the date, author, addressee or recipient, type of document, and name, address and telephone number of each person having possession, custody or control of the document or any copies of the document; and

(4) a payment of money, to state the person who made the payment, the person to whom. the payment was made, the date the payment was made, the amount of the payment, the purpose for which the payment was made and the manner of payment (e.g., by check, cash or wire).

(5) a statement or representation, to state the person who made the statement or representation, the person or persons to whom the statement or representation was made, the time when the statement or representation was made, the place where the statement or representation was made, the means by which the statement or representation was made (i.e., in person, by telephone, by letter) and the specific contents of the statement or representation.

ITEMS TO BE PRODUCED

REQUEST NO. 1. A certified copy of the policy, or policies, of insurance covering you and/or your agents while operating motor vehicles at the time and date of the subject incident, as well as the policy cover page, face page, or declaration page, including the limits of liability on all policies of insurance.

RESPONSE:

REQUEST NO. 2: Photographs or drawings of the scene of the collision, vehicles involved in said collision, or pertaining to the collision in any way.

RESPONSE:

REQUEST NO. 3. All internal memoranda, correspondence or other records regarding this incident, including any incident or risk manager reports.

RESPONSE:

REQUEST NO. 4: Any and all statements, including but not limited to those of the Plaintiff and Defendant, which have been taken regarding the subject incident.

RESPONSE:

REQUEST NO. 5: Any and all repair bills or estimates of repair regarding any vehicle involved in this collision.

RESPONSE:

REQUEST NO. 6: Any and all medical records of the Plaintiff in the possession of the Defendant.

RESPONSE:

REQUEST NO. 7: All documents which are generally or specifically identified in your answers to Interrogatories.

RESPONSE:

REQUEST NO. 8: The entire "driver file", employment file, or personnel file maintained for [Defendant driver].

RESPONSE:

SAMPLE REQUESTS FOR ADMISSIONS TO DEFENDANT IN PERSONAL INJURY (AUTO COLLISION) CASE

PLAINTIFFS' FIRST REQUESTFOR ADMISSIONS TO DEFENDANT

Come now the Plaintiffs, by counsel, and, pursuant to Trial Rule _____ of the [State} Rules of Procedure, request that the Defendant _____ respond fully to the following Request for Admissions, and return responses to the offices of _____ within thirty (30) days of service hereof.

DEFINITIONS

"Subject incident", "subject collision", and "collision" shall refer to the motor vehicle collision which occurred on [date] in _____ County, [State] which is the subject of this lawsuit.

"Driver" or "your driver" shall refer to the driver of your vehicle at the time of the subject incident.

REQUEST FOR ADMISSIONS

1.   The collision which is the subject of this lawsuit occurred on [date].

ANSWER:

2.   The collision which is the subject of this lawsuit occurred at [location].

ANSWER:

3. Immediately prior to this collision the vehicle driven by Defendant [Defendant driver] was traveling [direction] on [location].

ANSWER:

4. Immediately prior to this collision the vehicle driven by Plaintiff [Plaintiff] was traveling [direction] on [location].

ANSWER:

5. At the time of the collision, Defendant [Defendant driver] was acting within the course and scope of his employment as an agent, servant or employee of {Defendant driver's employer].

ANSWER:

6. At the time of the collision Defendant [Defendant driver] was driving under the direction and control of [Defendant driver's employer].

ANSWER:

7. Defendant [Defendant driver] was not acting as in independent contractor at the time of the collision.

ANSWER:

8. Defendant [Defendant driver's employer] paid Defendant [Defendant driver] wages, tips or other income while he was employed by [Defendant driver's employer].

ANSWER:

9. On [Date of incident] the vehicle driven by Defendant [Defendant driver] collided with the rear of the vehicle driven by Plaintiff [Plaintiff].

ANSWER:

10. The collision which is the subject of this lawsuit was caused by [Defendant driver].

ANSWER:

11. [Plaintiff] did nothing to cause this collision.

ANSWER:

12. [Plaintiff] could not have avoided this collision.

ANSWER:

13.   Immediately prior to this collision Defendant [Defendant driver] did not observe the Plaintiff's vehicle.

ANSWER:

14.   Defendant [Defendant driver] failed to drive his vehicle in a reasonably prudent manner.

ANSWER:

15.   Defendant [Defendant driver] was negligent in the operation of his vehicle and his negligence was the proximate cause of the collision.

ANSWER:

Index

Page numbers in *italics* refer to exhibits.